Book Cover by Philip Brian Tomlinson

1st edition 2024

Dedication

For Tess

This book is dedicated to Tess, and I hope that when we look back and connect the dots, the ripples this book sends into the world will reveal the significance of the 24-year chapter of my life we shared.

A Special Thank You

Rebecca Hart's influence has been transformative to the extent that this book feels like a shared creation. While the concepts are mine, Rebecca's editorial guidance, project management, and inspiration have been pivotal in bringing this work to life. Without her, I would likely procrastinate, endlessly tweaking rather than finishing.

Rebecca, I cannot thank you enough for believing in this book, sharing this vision, and pouring hours into making it what it is. This book is only here, polished and complete, because of you.

Guided by the Source

Your how-to guide

Philip Brian Tomlinson

Contents

Introduction 1

Part 1: Awakening to the Source

1. Shifting Perspectives: Viewing the World Anew #
2. Answering the Call to Write #
3. Discovering the Source: Guidance from Within #

Part 2: Understanding the Source and Our Connection

4. The Essence of Being: Origins of the Source #
5. The Journey Begins #

6. From Doubt to Faith #

Part 3: Aligning with the Source

7. Walking in Harmony with the Source #

8. Aligning with the Source #

9. Recognising the Gifts of the Source #

Part 4: Manifestation and Challenges

10. The Art of Contrast: Growth Through Life's Dualities #

11. Creating with Intention: Free Will and Manifestation #

12. Intention, Not Deed #

13. Breaking Free from Self-Fulfilling Prophecies #

14. Beyond Filters: Embracing Truth's Complexity #

Part 5: Practical Wisdom for Living with Purpose

15. Spilt Milk and New Beginnings #

16. The Indirect Path #

17. The Transformative Power of Gratitude #

18. Creating Ripples of Kindness #

19. Win When Nobody Else Loses #

Part 6: Tools for Reflection and Growth

20. The Weekly Compass #

21. A Guide to Daily, Weekly, and Monthly Reflection #

Part 7: Final Thoughts and Community

22. Expanding Beyond Filters #

23. A Final Reflection #

24. Joining the Guided by the Source Community #

Introduction

Welcome to a journey shaped by over thirty years of reflection, life lessons, and personal discoveries. This book is not a set of rigid rules or a mandate on what to believe.

Instead, it's a trusted companion on your path—a guide to help you navigate the complexities of life, understand the experiences that shape you, and feel supported in your personal exploration.

This book's inspiration was planted many years ago. Still, its roots dig much deeper, stretching through countless moments of seeking, discovering, and questioning.

I'm sharing the insights and reflections that have

resonated with me along the way. Some may also strike a chord with you, sparking ideas or shifting your perspective.

This book isn't about giving you the answers; it's about prompting you to find your own.

Here's how this book is structured to support that aim: at the end of some chapters, you'll find a reflection section. This is your opportunity to pause, process what you've read, and connect the ideas to your experiences.

Some chapters also include a brief exercise to help you deepen your understanding, whether through journaling, meditation, or simply observing something in your daily life.

These reflections and exercises are intended to take the concepts off the page and into your world, offering you a chance to apply them in a way that feels right for you.

I've designed this book with accessibility in mind, featuring slightly larger text, in-paragraph line breaks, and generous line spacing to make it easier for everyone to read. The ideas within are simple and approachable, crafted to ensure each chapter is something you can absorb and adapt to your needs. Take what resonates with you, leave what doesn't, and trust that your path will unfold uniquely.

I'm honoured to share this journey with you.

Part 1: Awakening to the Source

Shifting Perspectives: Viewing the World Anew

Shifting Perspectives: Viewing the World Anew

When I was 12, my parents took me to a child psychologist. Mind you, it was not their idea—the school had suggested it and set up the appointment, evidently concerned that my thinking was "abnormal." They'd noticed I wasn't strictly following the expected learning methods. Oh, I'd get the correct answers, just not how they wanted.

That day, I went through a series of tests—IQ tests, conversation-based evaluations, you name it.

The school had sent me off in hopes of diagnosing a learning difficulty. Instead, they received a diagnosis of sorts they hadn't anticipated.

The psychologist concluded that my brain wasn't malfunctioning; it was simply doing things differently, following its path through the forest of logic, intuition, and perhaps a bit of stubborn curiosity.

Since childhood, I've always had my way of doing things. When given a problem, I felt free not to follow the exact route laid out by others. I wanted to take my path and discover the "why" behind each step.

Why should I unquestioningly accept things as they were just because someone told me that's how they were meant to be?

Years later, my parents gave me the letter sent to them by the school psychologist. I was at the ceiling of some of those IQ tests. The psychologist told my parents that talking to me was like conversing with an adult; we even touched on deep philosophical concepts!

While having a high IQ sounds grand on paper, it's a mixed blessing. Like being able to see far off into the distance but sometimes missing the flowers blooming at your feet.

Being on the autistic spectrum meant I was wired to dig deep, examine the hidden layers and seek the "why" of everything. It's hard to disregard details when wired this way. I wasn't built for blind faith. Instead, I needed things to fit, to form a cohesive whole.

My mind was always seeking connections and explanations, which meant simple acceptance of anything was rare. But this tendency to question and to stray from convention has its upside—it's like carrying around a personalised map of life that occasionally reveals shortcuts and hidden paths others might miss.

A Journey Begins with Tea

Life has a funny way of setting us on unexpected

paths. In my case, it all began with a simple CB radio and, of course, a cup of tea. At 15, I stumbled upon the CB radio—a marvellous device that allowed me to chat with people far and wide.

Fast forward to my twenties, and I was still captivated by it. So, when I heard of someone advertising just the radio I was looking for, I couldn't resist. Little did I know that this seemingly routine purchase would change my life.

Arriving to collect the radio, I was greeted by Mick, who would become a lifelong friend. The transaction was quick, but in classic British fashion, he invited me in for a cup of tea. That cup of tea led me to Irene, Mick's wife, who had extraordinary gifts.

Irene's first words were a polite greeting; then she asked if she could share "evidence of the spirit world." Intrigued, I nodded, unaware that I was about to be launched down a spiritual rabbit hole.

As Irene began to reveal details about my life, I was transfixed. Her insights were uncannily accurate, right down to a trivial disagreement my partner and I had

had the night before about a new table's placement in the living room. (I insisted it go in the corner; they wanted it under the window.

Petty, yes, but that's the thing—she knew.) My mind whirled. How on earth did she know? I was hooked, and my curiosity ignited.

What began as a casual cup of tea became weekly sessions in Irene's spiritual development circles, where she helped others unlock their psychic and mediumship abilities. I even tried my hand at psychometry—reading personal objects to uncover insights about people.

Astonishingly, I was pretty good at it. Week after week, my understanding of the spiritual world deepened. Meditation was challenging for my overactive mind, but I kept going, learning, and questioning.

Breaking Free from Labels

It's funny how Life's most significant lessons often arrive through the most unexpected encounters. In my early twenties, late one night, I was tuned into my trusty CB radio when I heard a voice crackle through the airwaves, introducing himself as "FLG"—short for "Finger-Lickin' Good." Who could resist chatting with someone who dared to use that as a handle?

So, a casual conversation began, marking the start of one of the most transformative friendships of my Life.

After hours of chatting over the radio, Fred, the voice behind "FLG," eventually invited me for a cup of tea. Going from CB banter to a real-life cuppa felt odd, but something urged me to meet this man in person.

That single cup of tea turned into countless Saturday afternoons in his living room, where we'd talk for hours about Life, beliefs, and the "whys" of existence. As it turned out, Fred was a philosopher in his own right, with a perspective that could turn anyone's world on its head.

Fred didn't see the world as most people did and wasn't afraid to say so. He had an uncanny knack for questioning everything, and slowly but surely, he began "deprogramming" me. Every belief I'd held, every assumption I'd never asked—he challenged it all.

Were these my beliefs or hand-me-downs from society, religion, or even a well-meaning family? It was eye-opening. It was like seeing the world with fresh eyes.

One of Fred's most significant teachings was the importance of avoiding labels. He saw labels as rigid boxes that stifle our thinking. He explained that while we need words to communicate, we shouldn't let those words become the entire story.

For instance, when I use the term "God," I understand it's a loaded word that means different things to different people. For some, it's a figure in religious texts; for others, it's simply Life's essence. Fred urged me to dig deeper and question whether these terms were mine or just borrowed ideas.

So, in this book, I'll use "*the Source*" rather than "God." Why? Because *the Source*, at least as I see it, is the origin of all things—a concept free from any religious or cultural definition.

We can all relate to it, even if we interpret it differently. To me, it's the creative energy of the universe, the wellspring of existence. I can't claim to know what it is entirely, but I can share what resonates.

Similarly, "spirit" and "soul" often carry assumptions, So I'll share my take on this while encouraging you to develop yours. For me, the spirit is the unfiltered energy of *the Source* that exists within us, like a vial of pure essence.

It's always connected to *the Source*, but when this spirit becomes entangled in human experience, it forms our soul. In my view, the soul is a blend of our human experiences and our eternal spirit—a guide, nudging us when we're aligned with our purpose and giving us a prod when we're not.

As you read through this book, I invite you to let my words be stepping stones, not end-all definitions. Instead of taking these ideas at face value, let them unfold, see how they resonate, and feel free to reshape them if they don't fit.

Life isn't about rigidly sticking to the labels handed down to us. It's about peeling back those layers to uncover our truth and perhaps a deeper connection with *the Source*.

Answering the Call to Write

Finding Purpose Through Self-Expression

It was an ordinary Sunday evening when I attended our usual church service. I was seated in the congregation, listening to the philosophy shared before the mediumship demonstration. Then, the medium approached me, asking if she could work with me. I agreed, not thinking much of it, and she delivered a brief yet mysterious message: "Here is a pen—write the book."

I had yet to learn what she was talking about. I didn't think to ask, "What book?" I just thanked her politely, not wanting to reveal my confusion. I've always been one to help people grasp new ideas, often preferring to guide them toward their understanding. Still, the notion of writing a book was baffling.

The following week, I returned to church; this time, a different medium approached me. "They want you to write the book," she said, in a tone that left no room for misunderstanding. "You need to write it."

Once again, I thanked her and went home scratching my head, asking, "What book?" After all, my skills were primarily technical—computers, wiring, practical things. Nothing seemed to click.

I tried a different spiritualist church because I felt caught in a cosmic practical joke. Perhaps this particular message was tied to the first church, I thought. I sat at the back, hoping to evade further instructions from the spirit world. No luck.

With a wry smile, the medium spotted me and said, "You can hide all you like; they'll still find you. Write the book."

Determined to avoid further messages, I eventually stopped attending church. But no matter where I went, mediums kept popping up with the same instruction: "Write the book." One even told me, "This book will have a major impact."

By now, I was thoroughly spooked. But as time passed, I felt a strange, quiet shift—a growing sense that perhaps there *was* something I needed to say.

I've always been a good talker, able to communicate verbally without much fuss. Writing, however, felt like an entirely different beast. And here I am, speaking into my phone, letting it transcribe my words because writing still doesn't come naturally to me.

As I lie here in my campervan, recording these thoughts, I'm trusting that whatever comes out is precisely what's meant to be.

Now, why would *the Source* pick me to write a book? I'm no writer. My school years in English were nothing to boast about, and the idea of being a "writer" seemed laughable. But people often say I have a way of talking about spirituality that draws people in, like the Pied Piper.

Speaking is one thing; it's personal, interactive, spontaneous. Writing a book felt like jumping into the deep end without knowing where the bottom was.

Skip forward again to June 2024. I had finally decided that the book I should write is about my understanding of the truth of existence. At this time, I was on my way to Orkney with my friend Terry Smith to celebrate the summer solstice.

Just before we reached Orkney, Terry mentioned wanting to do something spiritual. We stumbled upon a mediumship demonstration at Kirkwall Theatre and went along with a few friends.

Before the event, Terry challenged me. "This is the perfect chance to have an unspoken question answered. You said you are being guided in writing the book, but the spirit won't identify who it is. Ask in your mind who's been guiding you spiritually," he said. "If this medium's any good, she can tell you."

Sure enough, the medium approached me during the show and began, "I have a man here—the tall one who was a sergeant major." She described him perfectly and said he was working with me.

She then mentioned, "You've been listening to an audiobook about writing on your way up here, haven't you?" Gobsmacked, I could only nod; I had been listening to a book on writing, trying to wrap my head around this task.

"You don't need that," she continued. "Everything you need to write this book is already inside you."

Then, to answer my unspoken question, she added, "An angel is working on the book with you." Though she didn't name this presence, she confirmed its angelic nature,

And so, here I am, still bewildered but following the call. *The Source* seems determined for this book to be written, so I press on, trusting that these words—however imperfect—are meant to be shared.

Discovering the Source: Guidance from Within

Unveiling the Source as Mentor and Companion

Introduction: Discovering the Source

Throughout cultures and centuries, humanity has sought to name and understand a force that connects, animates, and sustains everything. Some call it God, others the Universe, Spirit, or simply *the Source*.

This term—*the Source*—is used here to represent an energy that transcends cultural or religious boundaries. It is vast, boundless, and accessible, guiding and nurturing us as we navigate our journeys.

Unlike a person, *the Source* does not conform to human traits or rules. Instead, it is better understood as an infinite energy that flows through all things. By connecting with *the Source*, we gain insights into our place in the world and feel part of a greater universal whole.

Every experience and connection contributes to this intricate web of life, interwoven by *the Source*.

Guidance as a Mentor

When we open ourselves to *the Source*, we often experience a unique form of guidance—a gentle yet persistent influence that helps us align with our true path. Some experience this guidance as an inner mentor, an unseen presence that doesn't impose or dictate but subtly encourages introspection and discovery.

This guidance isn't an external teacher with fixed

lessons but rather an inner knowing that grows as we connect more deeply to our lives and purpose.

Such guidance doesn't present ready-made answers or clear instructions; it offers gentle nudges and quiet reminders, prompting us to look inward and find clarity within ourselves. It respects our free will, inviting us to use our experiences as the foundation for our choices.

Rather than mapping out a rigid path, this mentor allows us to seek and explore the direction that most resonates with our individual nature.

How the Source Communicates

The guidance from *the Source* is subtle, often arriving in unexpected ways. It might feel like a sudden insight, an intuitive nudge, or a sense that one path feels more "right" than another.

This guidance can reveal itself through life patterns or synchronicities—those seemingly coincidental moments that prompt us to consider a particular choice or perspective.

It may appear as a quiet, inner voice or intuition, helping us steer back on course if we've veered off.

This guidance from *the Source* has felt like a delicate dance between inner reflection and external signs. When I felt uncertain or struggled with decisions, the mentor within would offer calm reassurance, reminding me to trust in my journey.

Rather than imposing answers, this guidance helped me find the wisdom already within me, connecting my inner truth with the expansive energy of *the Source*.

The Nature of the Source as a Constant Presence

Imagine *the Source* as a vast ocean and each of us as individual waves moving within it. While each wave is distinct, it remains inseparably part of the ocean's entirety. *The Source* is the beginning, the end, and the expanse in between—a wellspring of creativity, love, and potential that flows through each of us.

It doesn't command our lives but quietly inspires growth, understanding, and unity.

This boundless energy is always present, surrounding and filling us, ready to guide anyone open to it. Tapping into *the Source* requires no complex rituals or rigid doctrines. Instead, it only asks for our presence, openness, and the willingness to trust in those quiet inner whispers that lead us forward.

Building a Relationship with *the Source*

Connecting with *the Source* doesn't mean surrendering control; instead, it is the beginning of a profound partnership. This relationship respects our free will, allowing us to explore our unique path while drawing on the vast, nurturing wisdom available.

Here are some simple practices that can help deepen this relationship:

•**Mindfulness**: By staying present, we become more attuned to the subtle guidance from *the Source.*

•**Gratitude**: Expressing gratitude lifts our spirit, aligning us with the abundant love flowing from *the Source.*

•**Reflection**: Reflecting on our thoughts and experiences deepens our awareness of how *the Source* is present.

•**Trusting Intuition**: Listening to and honouring our intuition strengthens our bond with *the Source*, helping us to make choices that resonate with our purpose.

Embracing the Mentor Within

The guidance we receive from *the Source* does not consist of strict directives but rather of encouraging us to approach life with curiosity, humility, and an open heart. Our experiences become the curriculum, and our choices form the lessons.

The mentor within us invites us to seek our own truths and stay aligned with our purpose.

Engaging with this gentle guidance teaches us to navigate life's complexities with grace and resilience. Each step forward, each challenge and triumph, brings us closer to understanding and aligning with *the Source*'s quiet but powerful presence.

Through this partnership, we can approach life wonderfully, knowing we are supported by something infinitely wise.

Reflection: Aligning with *the Source*

Take a few moments to reflect on your relationship with *the Source*. Have you ever felt a decision was guided or that certain events unfolded to lead you towards clarity? How did these insights shape your path?

Reflect on these moments as gentle reminders from *the Source*, encouraging you to trust in the journey, even when the path ahead is uncertain.

Part 2: Understanding the Source and Our Connection

The Essence of Being: Origins of the Source

Exploring the Birthplace of All Things

The origins of existence are notoriously tricky to explain—they lie beyond the boundaries of our reality and defy most of what we "know." Throughout history, humanity has developed mythological stories, religious narratives, and scientific theories to explain these origins.

From creation tales involving gods and angels to today's explorations in quantum theory and energy, our understanding of existence has evolved dramatically. One truth, however, remains constant: everything is energy, and energy doesn't end; it transforms.

Let me offer a simple analogy to make this concept more tangible. It's humanised, simplified, and only skims the surface of a much larger mystery, but it's one way to get closer to imagining where we come from and, perhaps, what we're here to do.

The Source and the Spirit

Imagine, if you will, a vast and boundless expanse of energy. This isn't just any energy—it's everything. Imagine it as an infinite pool stretching out endlessly. This pool is *the Source*—the origin, the beginning, and the foundation of all that exists.

Now, picture yourself standing at the edge of this pool with a glass bottle. You dip the bottle into the water, filling it to the brim. With a quick twist, you seal it with a transparent cap and toss it back into the pool. Here's the exciting bit: the water inside the bottle is the same as the water outside, but it's now enclosed.

That bottle represents a spirit—an individual form of *the Source's* energy. The bottle, now filled, remains submerged, indistinguishable from the water around it, yet it has a distinct "identity." Like the water in the bottle, a spirit is *the Source* encapsulated, always part of *the Source* but capable of unique experiences.

In this boundless pool are countless spirits—individualised forms of the same energy, forever connected within *the Source*. They're all in communion, sharing in the infinite power of *the Source*, yet each is on its journey, seeking to experience, learn, and grow.

The Book of the Spirit

Let's think of each spirit as carrying a "book." Every lifetime—every incarnation in the physical world—adds a new chapter to this book. The spirit's purpose, across countless lives, is to experience as much as possible. There's a significant difference between *knowing* something and *living* it.

For example, one thing is knowing the steps of skydiving—boarding the plane, leaping, feeling the rush of air, pulling the parachute, and landing safely. But the sheer thrill, the intense rush of emotions, the visceral experience? That's something else entirely.

In its infinite wisdom, *the Source* knows all there is to know. But it can feel these truths through us—our souls, lives and experiences. Each of our lives allows *the Source* to experience a different facet of existence. Through our unique experiences, especially those that have never been had before, new energy is created. *The Source* doesn't just expand—it evolves.

Reflection: Embracing Our Origins and Purpose

1. **Contemplating Connection**

The bottle within the pool analogy reminds us that while we may feel separate, we're actually part of something larger. Reflect on times when you felt an undeniable connection to something beyond yourself, whether through nature, art, or a shared moment. How might seeing yourself as part of *the Source's* evolution change your perspective on Life's challenges and joys?

2. **Living as a Vessel for Experience**

This chapter suggests our lives serve a purpose beyond our gain. Think about a challenge that profoundly changed you. How did it contribute to your growth? Imagine this growth as personal growth and as adding to a larger purpose for all existence.

3. **From Knowing to Experiencing**

The skydiving example underscores that proper understanding often comes through experience rather than knowledge. Think about an experience that changed your understanding of a concept, like trust or resilience. How might seeking new experiences deepen your insight into the mysteries of Life?

4. **Seeing Life as an Offering to *the Source***

This chapter proposes that our experiences contribute to *the Source's* growth. Consider what unique perspectives, strengths, or lessons you bring. How might embracing this idea encourage you to live more fully and boldly?

5. **Purpose Beyond the Self**

Seeing ourselves as vessels for *the Source* can shift how we view our lives. How does this perspective influence your daily Life, relationships, or goals? What small actions might you take to honour this sense of interconnected purpose?

Exercise: Mapping Your Spirit's Journey

Take a moment to sketch a timeline of your life, focusing on pivotal experiences, even if they were challenging. Start by marking out events or phases that have left a lasting impression on you—times when you felt a shift within, made a significant decision or found yourself facing something unexpected.

These key moments don't have to be dramatic. They could include subtle but powerful experiences like meeting someone who inspired you, discovering a hobby that made you feel alive, or even moving to a new place that changed your perspective.

As you go through your timeline, consider:

•**Turning Points**: Times when life felt like it veered in a new direction, such as a change in career, a new relationship, or a move. These could be moments of choice or necessity—any event that feels like it steered you onto a different path.

•**Periods of Challenge**: Moments of struggle, loss, or hardship that pushed you to grow or see life differently. Often, we face fears, losses, or trials that shape our resilience and compassion.

•**Moments of Joy or Passion**: Times when you felt deeply happy, engaged, or "in the flow." These can reveal your core passions, values, or experiences that energize your spirit.

•**Times of Reflection or Realisation**: Any quiet or unexpected moments that brought clarity or insight, such as a conversation that changed your perspective or a book that resonated with your soul.

•**Periods of Learning or Personal Growth**: Phases when exploring new skills, studying, or broadening your understanding of yourself and the world. These could involve formal learning or simply the valuable lessons life presents to you.

Next to each event, jot down a "chapter title" you'd give to that experience if it were part of your spirit's book. For example:

•**"The Courage to Begin Again"** for rebuilding after a setback.

•**"Discovering My Voice"** for a phase when you gained confidence in expressing your true self.

•**"Embracing the Unknown"** for a period when you took a leap of faith, even if it was scary.

•**"Lessons in Letting Go"** for an experience that taught you the power of release, such as moving on from an attachment or expectation.

•**"The Awakening Call"** For the first time, you felt drawn to explore spirituality or ask bigger questions about life's purpose.

As you review your timeline and these titles, see if any themes emerge. Do you notice patterns of resilience, growth, or learning that align with your spirit's journey, helping you see the purpose woven through your experiences?

In these reflections, we are invited to view Life as part of an ongoing journey with *the Source.* Each of our experiences is a small but meaningful contribution to the evolution of all existence. By embracing this perspective, we can approach Life with a greater sense of unity, gratitude, and openness—even to the parts that challenge or surprise us.

The Journey Begins

Following the Call of the Source

So here you are, newly born into the world. Once a spirit with vast, boundless knowledge, you've chosen to combine with a human body—a tiny, physical being with limited abilities and even less awareness of the universe's grand mysteries.

In this instant, your spirit transforms into a soul, and while keeping a connection to the wisdom of the past, you begin with a clean slate, ready for the learning, growing, and experiencing that life brings.

Early Years and Free Will in Waiting

In your first years, life is about following others'

guidance rather than expressing your free will. Parents or caregivers make most of the decisions—what you wear, where you go, how you spend each day. Yet, even at this stage, your soul has a presence, a purpose.

Although your role is small at first, these early years are essential to your journey.

The Source begins to nudge you toward specific interests. This could be a love for music, a fascination with colours, or an eagerness to dance. These nudges often appear as childhood passions, unique interests that bring you joy and a feeling of connection.

They're gentle signals from *the Source*, setting you on paths that may later reveal themselves as significant.

A Note for Parents: Encouraging Passion in Children

Your role is crucial here for parents or mentors in a child's life. When a child shows a natural love for something, whether drawing, dancing, or simply building blocks with wild enthusiasm, that excitement could spark their soul's calling.

Nurture these interests—your encouragement can have a lasting impact. By supporting a child's passion, you might align them with experiences or skills that will be crucial on their life path, helping them unlock parts of their soul's purpose even in their earliest years.

Stepping into Your Own Choices

As you grow older, you begin to step out into the world and make more decisions on your own. Now that you can act with intention, *the Source* will guide you even more closely if you're willing to listen.

Guidance from *the Source* often feels like intuition—a gentle nudge to take a particular path, a gut feeling that pulls you toward one choice over another. These aren't random emotions or whims; they're subtle, wise sensations that encourage you to move in the best way that serves your soul's journey.

The more you pay attention to these feelings, the clearer and stronger they become. Like any muscle, the more you use your intuition, the better it works, and soon enough, you'll rely on it as a trusted guide.

Childhood as a Foundation

Childhood is a preparation period, a time to lay down roots, form early experiences and gather the first memories that will build into the adventure of your life. It's a chapter of learning, discovery, and formation, setting the stage for what's to come.

As you leave Childhood, you step more fully into your ability to make free, intentional choices, shaping your unique path.

Reflection: Embracing the Foundations of Our Soul's Journey

1. **Fresh Start, New Path**

Being born is a fresh start for the soul, a gift that allows you to experience life unfiltered and new. Consider your own beginnings and early memories—are there childhood dreams or interests that still resonate with who you are today?

2. **Guidance of *the Source***

The Source guides us, often subtly, even when we're

young. Reflect on moments from your Childhood when a particular activity or interest seemed to draw you in. Are there any threads that connect your younger self to your present-day passions?

3. **Supporting Children's Unique Gifts**

For those with children, this chapter emphasises the impact of nurturing a child's unique passions. Reflect on ways you can encourage children to explore what excites them. This support could be pivotal, gently nudging them toward the skills and experiences their soul seeks.

4. **Listening to Your Intuition**

As we grow, intuition becomes a powerful guide. Reflect on times when you've followed a "gut feeling" or inner nudge, and the outcome was meaningful. How might trusting and acting on your intuition strengthen this connection even further?

5. **Seeing Childhood as a Foundation**

Childhood is a foundational chapter in your soul's journey. Look back at the formative experiences that shaped you. Were there lessons, people, or challenges that became crucial stepping stones for your growth?

6. **Embracing Evolution Beyond the Foundations**

Childhood is just the beginning. Consider how far you've come since those early days and how the foundations set then have shaped your journey. As you move forward, keep those early interests in mind—are there any dreams or passions that still hold meaning and may hint at your unique path?

By understanding Childhood as both a blank canvas and a formative period, we can appreciate the beauty of the journey ahead. Each step in life, no matter how small or seemingly insignificant, has its role in shaping the grander path of your soul's calling.

With patience, trust, and openness to guidance, you're prepared to step boldly into this adventure, knowing that inner wisdom and the invisible hands of *the Source* support you.

From Doubt to Faith

Cultivating Intention and Inner Trust

Why doesn't *the Source*—the essence of existence—reveal itself as clearly as the sun in the sky? If it were so visible, would we even need faith? Why do we carry doubt in our hearts while seeking truth? These are questions that have puzzled seekers for centuries.

Yet doubt, as frustrating as it may feel, has a profound purpose. It completes our spiritual evolution. Just as light and shadow bring a painting to life, our spiritual growth is enriched by both certainty and doubt. Faith and doubt are partners, not opposites, in our journey.

The Role of Doubt in Life's Hardships

Life is filled with challenges for many. People around the world endure profound suffering—whether through poverty, illness, or heartbreak. In moments of despair, many might wish to escape the pain.

If *the Source* made itself known so clearly that all doubt vanished, people might leave their lives prematurely to return to that all-encompassing warmth. But our lives, even the painful moments, hold purpose.

Our incarnations aren't meant to be all light and ease; they're designed for the full spectrum of experiences. Even when facing unbearable hardships, our souls choose these journeys for the lessons they bring. Just as darkness adds depth to a painting, the shadows in our lives give greater meaning to the light.

These problematic moments help us understand compassion, empathy, and resilience.

Embracing Contrast

Perhaps in past lifetimes, you've experienced gentle, joy-filled journeys. Now, you might be here to live a challenging life that tests your resilience and brings you face-to-face with hardship. This is the beauty of contrast. As difficult as it is to accept, life's darker chapters allow us to see the light differently.

Faith would lose its significance without a doubt. If we knew everything for sure, if *the Source* were visible, then belief, trust, and hope would have no space to grow. Faith, in its most accurate form, is the bridge between doubt and knowing.

Light and Shadow

Some people feel a calling to shine their light into the world, hoping to dispel darkness wherever they go. Yet the brighter we shine, the more visible the shadows we cast.

Trying to force away the darkness around us can

sometimes lead to overwhelming feelings, yet it's all part of our journey.

Doubt doesn't negate faith; it strengthens it. Because of doubt, we can build resilience, practice trust, and learn the true nature of hope. Faith isn't the absence of doubt—it's choosing to believe in *the Source* even when the path ahead is shrouded in mist.

My Journey with Faith

In my own life, I've come to trust *the Source's* guidance, often revealed through intuition, subtle signs, and inspired thoughts. Of course, there are moments of doubt, but by listening and following those nudges, I've seen that even the most challenging paths lead to growth and understanding.

This trust in the unseen, in the gentle direction of *the Source*, has shown me that faith isn't about having all the answers but knowing *the Source* is always with us, even in silence.

Whatever challenge you face, remember: *the Source*

is aware of you. You are seen, heard, and loved. Even if it doesn't always feel this way, know that your journey has meaning and purpose. Doubt may cloud your vision, but it's through this fog that faith becomes more robust.

Reflection: Strengthening Faith Through Embracing Doubt

1. **Doubt as a Catalyst for Growth**

This chapter shows us that doubt isn't a barrier; it's a stepping stone. Just as shadows enhance a painting, doubt adds depth to faith. Reflect on times in your life when uncertainty tested you. How did these experiences strengthen your resilience or deepen your faith?

Embrace doubt as an essential part of spiritual growth, allowing it to lead you to greater understanding.

2. **Seeing Contrast as a Source of Wisdom**

Life's contrasts—light and shadow, joy and sorrow—give us perspective. Each problematic moment can deepen our appreciation for life's blessings. Think about a challenging period in your life. How did it change your perspective, shape your understanding, or increase your compassion?

Embracing both the highs and lows can make even the most challenging experiences feel purposeful.

3. **Faith Beyond Certainty**

Faith isn't about a lack of doubt; it's about moving forward despite it. Consider moments when you took a step into the unknown, guided by hope or intuition. These are moments where faith truly shines. Reflect on times you continued forward without certainty, leaning on inner trust.

Recognise these experiences as the roots of faith, growing stronger each time we choose belief over doubt.

4. **Recognising *the Source's* Subtle Guidance**

Even when we feel disconnected, *the Source* guides us in subtle ways. Reflect on "coincidences" or intuitive nudges leading you down the right path. These moments are reminders of *the Source's* presence.

Consider ways to strengthen your connection through quiet meditation, gratitude, or simply inviting *the Source* into your life's journey.

5. **Building Resilience Through Trust**

By embracing doubt, we cultivate a grounded, resilient form of trust. When facing uncertainty, remember that resilience isn't about constantly feeling confident; it's about moving forward, even with doubt as a companion.

How might accepting the unknown, even if it's unsettling, strengthen your resilience? In facing life's uncertainties, we open ourselves to unexpected growth.

Exercises: Navigating Faith and Doubt

Exercise 1: Embracing Doubt as a Teacher

•Spend a few quiet moments each day reflecting on areas of doubt in your life. Please write down the fears or questions clouding your faith, noting how they make you feel.

•Instead of resisting these doubts, ask yourself, "What can I learn from this uncertainty?" Embrace doubt as a teacher, allowing it to reveal aspects of yourself you may not have noticed before.

Exercise 2: Recognising the Role of Contrast

•Take time to think about recent moments of light and dark in your life. Write down contrasting experiences like joy, sorrow, or comfort and discomfort.

•Reflect on how each has contributed to your growth or understanding. Let this practice remind you that every shade of experience contributes to your unique journey.

Exercise 3: Building Faith Through Action

•List three ways you can strengthen your faith, even amid doubt. This might be through meditation, spending time in nature, practising gratitude, or intending to notice guidance from *the Source*.

•Choose one of these practices to integrate into your daily routine, noticing how it affects your sense of faith and inner peace over time.

Exercise 4: Strengthening Resilience with Affirmations

•Write affirmations acknowledging doubt and faith, such as "I trust in the process, even when I cannot see the outcome," or "I embrace uncertainty, knowing it's part of my journey."

•Repeat these affirmations daily, using them as gentle reminders to strengthen resilience and cultivate trust in the unfolding of your path.

Exercise 5: Connecting with *the Source* Through Conversation

•Each evening, spend a few moments conversing with *the Source*, expressing your intentions, concerns, and hopes. Invite *the Source's* presence into your life, even if it's felt only as a whisper.

•End by expressing gratitude, trusting that *the Source* listens and guides you, even when doubt lingers. Over time, this ritual can deepen your awareness of *the Source's* subtle presence.

Moving Forward: Doubt as the Soil for Faith

This chapter encourages us to welcome doubt as an ally rather than an enemy. Faith isn't about certainty but the courage to move forward, embracing both light and shadow. Doubt sharpens our faith, pushing us to seek *the Source's* guidance while accepting that not everything can be known.

With each step, remind yourself that you're never truly alone. In moments of uncertainty, trust that *the*

Source's presence surrounds you, guiding you through the unseen. Embrace the journey with open arms, knowing that every question and every answer are all part of the path leading you home.

Part 3: Aligning with the Source

Walking in Harmony with the Source

Finding Balance on the Path of Resonance

In the beginning—before beginnings, really—there was an energy, boundless and pure, a love without condition that I like to call *the Source*. Some call it God, the Universe, or simply "Nature." The words we choose are unimportant, but they're also loaded.

The word "God" alone can mean something entirely different from one person to another. Labels, with all their associations and beliefs, can sometimes get in the way of what we're trying to describe.

So, in this book, I'll refer to this vast energy as *the Source*. It's a term that feels freeing to me, a word that doesn't rely on any particular culture, tradition, or religion. But, of course, use any term that resonates with you.

What matters here is not the name itself but the connection and meaning it brings into our lives.

Discovering What Resonates

But how do you know if this idea of *the Source*, or anything else, really resonates with you? Quite simply, you'll feel it. It's not about logic or convincing; it's more like a quiet inner "yes."

When something aligns with our profound truths, we feel it in a way that goes beyond understanding—it's an inner harmony that can't easily be shaken.

As you review this book, please note any ideas that strike this kind of chord. Grab a notebook and jot down anything that feels true, meaningful, or worth exploring.

You might even consider it your own "Book of Beliefs"—a collection of insights that speak to your journey and help you develop a personal understanding of life and spirit.

Remember: Beliefs Are Meant to Evolve

Now, I don't expect you to agree with everything here. If I'd read this book five or ten years ago, there would be plenty I wouldn't have agreed with! Our beliefs are more like rivers than stones; they flow, shift, and adapt as our lives and experiences change.

What feels right today might evolve tomorrow, and that's a good thing.

As you read, take what resonates, leave what doesn't, and remember this is your unique journey. This isn't a rigid set of answers; it's a companion for your path, wherever that may lead. And if, one day, you find yourself rethinking ideas that once felt rock-solid, know that this evolution is all part of the journey.

Reflection: Exploring *the Source* and Resonance

1. **Moving Beyond Labels**

Just like "God" or "Source" carry layers of meaning, often shaped by personal and cultural beliefs. Reflect on your names or symbols for *the Source*. How do they shape your understanding?

Does reframing the energy as "*the Source*" help you connect in a way that feels less limited by past definitions?

2. **Listening to Inner Resonance**

Sometimes, ideas and beliefs resonate with us beyond words, giving us an inner "yes." Think of moments when you've felt this kind of alignment. What concepts or beliefs may have struck that chord within you?

Let this feeling guide you as you explore new ideas in this book and beyond.

3. **Creating a "Book of Beliefs"**

Consider starting your collection of insights and beliefs that feel true to your core. Use this opportunity to journal or note down ideas that resonate deeply. What themes or patterns emerge?

How does having a personal journal for your spiritual journey make you feel?

4. **Embracing a Shifting Path**

As my understanding of *the Source* has evolved, reflect on how your beliefs have changed. What once felt true but has since shifted?

5. **Opening to Diverse Beliefs**

We grow by remaining open to beliefs different from our own. Reflect on a time when a new perspective expanded your view.

How might curiosity toward others' beliefs deepen your spiritual journey?

6. **Spiritual Growth Through Life Events**

Experiences, insights, and relationships shape our beliefs. Consider a recent experience that's influenced your beliefs about *the Source*.

How can such moments help you continue evolving?

Exercise: Mapping Your Beliefs

Take a few minutes to map out ideas about *the Source*, spirit, and life's purpose. Draw a mind map or jot down words or phrases that come to mind. Don't censor yourself—just let it flow. Once finished, step back and notice any patterns or insights that surprise you.

These reflections and exercises invite you to connect deeply with your inner sense of what feels right. By letting go of labels, embracing resonance, and allowing for growth, you can begin building a spiritual path that's true to you. This journey is yours alone, unfolding in its own time and form.

Aligning with the Source

Manifesting from your Soul

As you live this life, *the Source* provides you with the experiences your soul seeks. When we talk about manifesting or calling things into our lives, it's essential to understand the difference between what our *soul* and mind want.

While the mind may wish for shiny distractions or quick fixes, the soul resonates with experiences that lead to growth, joy, and fulfilment. And it's the soul's Resonance that *the Source* hears and responds to.

As a part of *the Source,* your soul has a direct line to this ultimate energy. When it resonates with an experience it truly craves, it sends out a clear, vibrant signal, like a beacon calling *the Source* to assist in making it happen.

If there's something you sincerely wish to experience, trust that it is this Resonance—this true calling of your soul—that activates the process with *the Source*.

Soul Desires vs. Mind Desires

A critical piece in aligning with *the Source* is distinguishing between soul and mind desires. Imagine, for instance, that your mind wants financial wealth. But what if your soul is less concerned with money and more focused on the experiences wealth might bring—like freedom, creativity, or the peace of living in harmony with nature?

The Source doesn't respond to the specifics of "winning the lottery" but to the more profound experiences of freedom, connection, and joy that your soul resonates with.

When we concentrate on the experience and feelings we want rather than the specific form it might take, we give *the Source* the freedom to respond in unexpected and often more fitting ways. Focus on what brings you true joy and fulfilment, trusting that *the Source* will arrange the rest.

Later, I'll walk you through practical steps to strengthen this Resonance, helping you align more clearly with your soul's desires.

Reflection: Understanding and Aligning with Soul-Driven Desires

1. **Soul vs. Mind Desires**

Reflect on your current goals or aspirations. Are the pursuits of the mind motivated by societal expectations or surface-level desires? Or are they rooted in your soul's more profound calling for purpose, love, or growth?

Consider how focusing on soul-driven desires might bring a more fulfilling path forward.

2. **Manifesting Feelings, Not Things**

Think about the life experiences that resonate most deeply with you. Rather than focusing on material goals like a new car or house, imagine the feelings or lifestyle they represent—freedom, connection, or a sense of adventure.

What emotions or life experiences do you want to attract, and how might they align with your highest self?

3. **Finding Resonance with** *the Source*

Reflect on moments where you felt aligned with a sense of purpose or joy. How did that inner alignment shape your life?

Tuning into these moments strengthens your connection to *the Source*, and recognising them helps you follow similar paths that bring alignment.

4. **Trusting *the Source's* Response**

The Source often responds in ways that may not align with our immediate expectations. Think back to times when an unexpected outcome turned out to be beneficial. How might you embrace an open-hearted approach, trusting that *the Source* knows what best serves your journey?

5. **Aligning Intentions with Core Values**

Deep Resonance occurs when our goals reflect our soul's core values. Reflect on values that deeply resonate with you—such as love, peace, or creativity. How can aligning your intentions with these values lead to more meaningful experiences?

6. **Examining Superficial vs. Soulful Fulfillment**

Are there areas in your life where external success has left you unfulfilled? Reflect on how shifting focus to experiences that nourish your spirit might bring more enduring satisfaction and growth.

7. **Techniques for Soul-Source Resonance**

Consider meditation, journaling, or visualisation to deepen your connection with your inner self and clarify your soul's desires. Let these reflections serve as a foundation, preparing you for practical techniques to enhance your connection with *the Source*.

Focusing on what resonates with your soul rather than what might gratify your mind strengthens your alignment with *the Source*.

Trust that as you pursue these authentic experiences, *the Source* will respond in its way and time, offering guidance, connections, and opportunities that fit with your true path. In surrendering to this process, you open yourself to a life that reflects your soul's essence, supported at every step.

Recognising the Gifts of the Source

Opening to the Possibilities Along the Way

The Source brings us life experiences through opportunities, moments woven into our paths not by chance but by a deeper orchestration. *The Source* facilitates these opportunities through people who, inspired by nudges from their intuition, align with our soul's journey.

This isn't magic or divine intervention in a way that breaks reality's natural rules but rather a gentle influence that honours free will and maintains balance in the universe.

Many souls, particularly those who have lived through countless lifetimes, return to be facilitators for others, using their intuition to act as channels for opportunities that resonate with others' journeys.

Often, these souls aren't famous figures or spiritual leaders; they might be in positions where they make big or small decisions that open doors for others. Just as the intuition of these older souls guides them to be facilitators, other people's intuition might guide them to create opportunities for you, just as you may unwittingly create for them.

What feels like a coincidence could be an aligned moment set in motion by *the Source*.

Spotting Your "Red Cars"

Recognising these opportunities is essential. This is where the "red car" analogy comes into play. Imagine I asked you how many red cars you've seen today. You may not be able to recall a single one. But if I offered £10 for every red car you noticed, you'd suddenly see them everywhere.

This happens because our minds filter out much of what we don't actively focus on, missing things right before us. Our awareness expands when we shift our focus to see "red cars"—or opportunities.

The Source often presents us with opportunities, like "red cars", to guide our path, but we must stay alert to notice them. This focused awareness keeps us attuned to synchronicities, helping us better recognise opportunities in the present moment.

Exercise: Spotting "Red Cars" in Your Life

1. **Daily "Red Car" Focus**

Each morning, choose something to look out for during your day. This could be smiles from strangers, inspiring phrases, or spontaneous encounters.

This will help you see these "red cars" as opportunities from *the Source*.

2. **Record and Reflect**

At the end of each day, jot down any instances that match your focus. Did you feel nudged toward something new?

Were there moments that seemed too coincidental? Reflect on these observations to become more aware of how *the Source* subtly guides your path.

3. **Notice Patterns**

After a week, look at your notes to see if any themes or repeating signs emerge. Are certain types of opportunities consistently showing up?

This could be a hint from *the Source* about the direction your soul is seeking to go.

Crossroads and Free Will

The Source respects our free will, often presenting us with multiple opportunities simultaneously, each pointing slightly differently. Some may guide you toward your soul's desires, while others might be appealing distractions.

This way, choosing an opportunity becomes an act of free will rather than feeling like there's only one "right" choice.

Choosing can sometimes feel overwhelming,

especially when faced with two seemingly good options. But here's what I've learned: instead of agonising over which path is "correct," consider each option carefully. Visualise the outcomes, feel them out, and trust your intuition.

Choose the most exciting one, and commit fully to that choice. Even if it turns out to be a detour, *the Source* will present you with new opportunities. Every step, even the missteps, contributes to your soul's growth.

Exercise: Navigating Life's Crossroads with Intuition

1. **Visualise Each Path**

When you face a choice, take a few minutes to visualise the journey each path might offer. Imagine where each choice could lead you in six months or a year.

Notice how each option feels—is there one that resonates more profoundly or excites you?

2. **Ask for Guidance from *the Source***

Once you've visualised the options, sit in a moment of stillness, focusing on your intuition, and ask *the Source* for clarity. This can take any form you're comfortable with—meditation, a quiet walk, or journaling.

Let *the Source's* guidance emerge from within, often felt as a subtle knowing.

3. **Make a Choice and Commit**

Once you feel aligned with a choice, commit to it wholeheartedly.

Trust that even if the path isn't perfect, it's a step forward, and *the Source* will provide new crossroads as needed.

Embracing Rolling Roadblocks

Another concept that can help you navigate life's opportunities is "rolling roadblocks."

Imagine driving on the motorway in the UK, where a rolling roadblock might be set up to clear debris from the lanes.

A vehicle slows down traffic to allow a temporary,

clear space, keeping everyone safe.

When the obstacle is removed, the roadblock is lifted, and traffic flows smoothly again.

These rolling roadblocks might come in life as delays, setbacks, or moments where we feel stuck. Instead of seeing these as mere annoyances, consider that they might be designed to slow you down, aligning you to the right place at the right time.

The Source, respecting our reality's natural laws, sometimes needs time to bring all elements together, like the right people or setting, to create your opportunity.

These delays can ensure that you don't miss a pivotal moment, nudging you towards divine timing.

Exercise: Reframing Delays as Divine Timing

1. **Pause and Reflect**

When you encounter a delay or setback, instead of reacting with frustration, take a moment to pause. Ask yourself, "Is this roadblock slowing me down for a reason?"

Write down your reflections, noting any insights about how this delay might benefit you.

2. **Look for Synchronicity**

Often, setbacks lead to unexpected encounters or insights. During this time, pay attention to new people, ideas, or opportunities.

Consider that these might be part of a larger plan, perfectly timed to align with your journey.

3. **Gratitude for the Present**

Embracing a rolling roadblock means finding peace with being in the "waiting room." List three things you're grateful for in the present moment, even if they seem unrelated.

This helps you stay open to new possibilities and shifts your focus to what you can appreciate now.

Recognising Divine Timing

Consider moments in your life where things felt timed just right—those serendipitous encounters or perfect opportunities that arrived when you least expected them. Looking back, it's often easy to see how inevitable delays or detours led you to the right place at the right time.

The Source orchestrates these moments, aligning them with your soul's journey. This chapter encourages a mindset shift, embracing setbacks as potential blessings that guide us toward what's truly meant for us.

You can better align with *the Source's* flow by staying alert to these red cars, trusting your intuition at life's crossroads, and reframing delays as divine timing. Each step, even the unexpected ones, serves your path, allowing you to live purposefully and open-heartedly.

Part 4: Manifestation and Challenges

The Art of Contrast: Growth Through Life's Dualities

Learning from Light and Shadow on the Path

Imagine this: before embarking on your human journey, you—yes, the real you, the spirit—sat down to consider all the experiences you'd want to collect in this lifetime.

Each experience would be a valuable piece of understanding, fitting together like chapters in a massive, endless storybook of your soul. And *the Source* took note of it all, ready to nudge you when needed.

The Power of Contrast

Now, here's where it gets interesting. It might seem logical to think we'd all opt for only positive experiences, steering clear of the heartaches and rough patches. But here's the twist: to truly understand the richness of life, our spirits choose a balance of light and dark. That's the essence of contrast.

Consider contrast as life's bold strokes—those moments defining the extremes. It's like a painter using light and shadow to give depth to an image. We learn the profound joy of love only because we've felt loneliness.

We appreciate success because we've tasted failure. We gain a deeper, more vivid understanding of life through these highs and lows. Each extreme shapes us in ways that comfort alone never could.

So, when facing life's intense moments, remember: they're all essential strokes on the canvas of your soul's journey.

Navigating Life with Intuition

You might wonder, "How on earth am I supposed to navigate this maze of experiences?" Well, you're not without tools. Intuition is the inner compass guiding you through, the voice of your soul nudging you forward.

Listening to this voice connects you with the wisdom of *the Source*—urging you to take the leap, make the turn, or sometimes pause and reflect.

Tuning into your intuition may feel like a small step, but each step adds up. The more you trust and follow it, the more aligned you become with the path you set out to explore. The fantastic thing is that your intuition grows stronger as you use it.

As you develop this inner guidance, you move through life's contrasts with a greater sense of purpose.

Trusting the Adventure

This journey—complete with highs and lows,

twists and turns—is uniquely yours. Trust that every experience, even those that push you to the edge, is a part of your chosen life for your spirit's growth.

Embrace the contrasts as you walk your path, letting each moment add to the richness of your journey.

Reflection: Seeing Contrast as Life's Artful Brushstrokes

1. **Seeing Contrast as Life's Teacher**:

Reflect on the contrasts in your life, whether joy and sorrow or success and struggle. How have these extremes taught you more about yourself or reshaped your perspective?

What lessons might they be offering?

2. **Viewing Experiences as Purposeful Choices**:

Imagine the challenges in your life as purposefully chosen experiences.

How could viewing them in this way help you approach difficulties with a little more acceptance or even curiosity?

3. **Recognising Guidance When Needed**:

Have you ever felt supported by an unseen force or subtle intuition guiding you?

Reflect on moments when this inner nudge helped you or changed your path. How can trusting in this support make navigating challenges feel more manageable?

4. **Intuition as Life's Quiet Compass**:

Consider how often you listen to your intuition. Could paying more attention to those gut feelings guide you more confidently through the contrasts in your life?

Consider a recent decision—how did it feel to follow (or ignore) your intuition?

5. **Appreciating Life's Extremes**:

Moments of darkness and light enrich our human experience, helping us understand love, empathy, and resilience more deeply.

Reflect on how moments of struggle have given you a greater appreciation for joy or love. What insights can you carry forward?

6. **Trusting the Path Without Knowing the Destination**:

Sometimes, the path unfolds only as we walk it. Reflect on a time you trusted a path without a clear outcome.

How did it help you grow, and how could you bring more trust and patience to your current journey?

7. **Embracing Each Chapter of the Soul's Journey**:

Imagine each experience as a chapter in the story of your soul. What lessons or themes have emerged from recent chapters?

How might reframing these moments as purposeful lessons change your perspective?

Through these reflections, allow yourself to see contrast not as disruption but as essential to your chosen journey.

Embrace it as part of life's artistry, knowing that every twist and turn brings you closer to the soul's wisdom.

Trust in the journey, and let the full range of life's experiences shape you.

Creating with Intention: Free Will and Manifestation

The Balance of Choice and Guidance

Much has been shared about the law of attraction—an idea that it will eventually come to you if you think intensely about something. Many people imagine it operates like a natural law akin to gravity.

However, while gravity is a true force of nature within our universe, the manifestation process is more of a spiritual law governed by *the Source*. It exists outside the physical rules of our reality.

This distinction is essential because the law of attraction isn't a "law" in the strictest sense but rather a mechanism through which *the Source* aligns experiences with our soul's desires.

Our universe works within a framework of rules that *the Source* respects. If manifestation worked like magic, it would ignore these rules and infringe upon free will, a fundamental principle of our existence.

This means that while your soul can indeed experience the life it desires, it won't do so by magically bending reality. Instead, *the Source* orchestrates a series of opportunities that bring you closer to these experiences.

By focusing on the feelings behind what you desire rather than just the thing itself, you align with this process more naturally and powerfully.

The Power of Experience Over Possession

Rather than instantly granting material possessions, *the Source* aligns with your soul's desire to *experience* those things. For instance, you might focus on owning a red sports car.

But instead of one appearing on your driveway, an unexpected opportunity might arise to spend a day driving that car at a racetrack. Why? Because it's not about the car itself—it's about fulfilling your soul's experience of freedom, excitement, or joy.

Once you experience it, you've satisfied that soul-level desire and are ready to move on to new experiences.

Or take the example of dreaming about a beautiful home. Your soul may attract an invitation to stay in a stunning villa during a holiday. Working through the law of attraction, *the Source* grants you this chance to enjoy the beauty, peace, and comfort your soul craves, even if it's not permanent ownership.

Shinies and Their Temporary Appeal

We all have temporary desires, which I call "shinies" (pronounced Shynees). These are the thrill-seeking experiences that dazzle briefly before losing their appeal. For example, the joy of driving a new sports car may wear off.

Understanding the difference between shinies and true desires can help you focus your energy on experiences that bring lasting joy.

While being drawn to shinies is normal, fulfilling your soul's desires requires distinguishing between fleeting thrills and genuine long-term fulfilment. The latter is where your true manifestation power lies.

The Three Key Steps to Manifesting with the Source

So, how do you actively participate in manifesting with *the Source*?

Here are three foundational steps to bring your desires to life, focusing on the experiences your soul craves.

Step One: Feel the Experience

1. **Visualise with Emotion**

The first step is to experience your desire

emotionally and mentally, imagining it as vividly as possible. If you want a home by the sea, close your eyes and imagine every detail. Feel the joy of walking into the house, smelling the ocean air, and sipping coffee on your balcony.

Engage your senses and allow yourself to feel grateful for it as if it's already part of your reality.

2. **Set Regular Moments for Visualisation**

Try visualising just before sleep or during quiet moments throughout the day.

Falling asleep with your desires in mind can help embed them deeply within your subconscious, aligning your spirit more closely with these experiences.

3. **Practice Daytime Visualisations**

Even during busy days, find a few moments to recall your desired experiences, even briefly.

This keeps your desires active and maintains your connection with *the Source's* energy.

Exercise: Daily Visualisation Practice

•Set aside five minutes each morning or evening to immerse yourself in a specific experience you wish to manifest.

Feel the emotions you associate with this experience—peace, happiness, excitement.

•After each session, express gratitude as if you've already had the experience.

This shifts your energy, aligning it with the feeling of already living your desires, a powerful way to attract similar energy from *the Source*.

Step Two: Look for Opportunities

Opportunities appear as synchronicities, chance meetings, or ideas that pop up suddenly.

These are not random; they are intentional cues from *the Source*, helping you move towards your experiences.

1. **Stay Open to the Unexpected**

Like the red car theory, look for signs and synchronicities related to your desire.

The more attention you pay, the more you'll notice these nudges from *the Source*. This heightened awareness allows you to catch opportunities you might otherwise miss.

2. **Use Intuition as Your Compass**

As these opportunities arise, tune into your intuition. You may feel a subtle excitement or a "gut feeling" that urges you to act.

Your spirit resonates with the opportunity presented, helping you navigate easily.

Exercise: Spotting Synchronicities

•Each evening, write down any unusual events, chance encounters, or "coincidences" you noticed during the day. Reflect on how they might connect with your desires.

•After a week, look for any patterns in these occurrences. This can help you intuitively understand how *the Source* guides you through everyday life.

Step Three: Release Attachment to the Outcome

One of manifestation's most challenging yet essential aspects is releasing attachment.

By letting go of rigid expectations, you allow *the Source* to deliver the best version of your desire—even if it looks different than you imagined.

1. **Trust the Process**

Embrace patience and trust that *the Source* works, even if results aren't immediate.

Holding on too tightly to specific outcomes can create resistance, blocking the flow of manifestation.

2. **Celebrate the Journey**

Every step, success or setback, brings you closer to understanding and fulfilling your soul's desires.

Embrace each experience as a stepping stone rather

than fixating on one goal.

Exercise: Letting Go Meditation

•Take a few moments each day to sit quietly and focus on releasing any attachment to a specific outcome.

•Inhale deeply, feeling gratitude for your desire, and exhale to let go, trusting that *the Source* is guiding you.

Reflection: Harnessing the Law of Attraction with Awareness and Alignment

1. **Understanding Manifestation Beyond Materialism**

Reflect on past experiences where you focused intensely on wanting an experience rather than a material item. How did it affect the outcome?

When setting intentions, think about shifting focus to the feeling or experience rather than the object itself.

2. **Distinguishing True Desires from Temporary Thrills**

Consider desires you once chased that now feel unimportant. How can you distinguish between a genuine soul desire and a temporary "shiny"?

In the future, focus on desires that resonate deeply and bring lasting joy.

3. **Staying Open to Synchronicities**

Reflect on when synchronicities or chance encounters lead you closer to your goals. How can you maintain awareness of these signs?

Practising this awareness can enhance your sensitivity to *the Source's* guidance.

4. **Embracing Patience and Releasing Expectations**

Think about a time when you released a specific outcome and instead enjoyed the journey. How did letting go change your experience?

Practice surrendering to *the Source's* timing, knowing each step is crucial to the larger picture.

Moving Forward with Manifestation

Manifestation is an unfolding journey, not a one-time wish-granting session. By experiencing your desires, noticing *the Source's* subtle cues, and trusting in divine timing, you allow life to flow naturally towards your soul's experiences.

With these steps, you're not just passively waiting for things to happen; you're engaging in a dynamic alignment with *the Source*, creating a life rich with meaning, growth, and fulfilment.

Intention, Not Deed

Understanding the Intention Behind the Action

In life, it's easy to feel hurt or frustrated by the actions of others, especially when their behaviour seems careless or unkind. We often fixate on the act itself—the deed—and how it has affected us.

However, if we can take a step back and consider the intention behind the action, we might find a different perspective. Often, people don't intend to cause harm; they act in the way they feel is best, based on their own experiences, limitations, and understanding.

To illustrate this idea, let me share a story.

The Story of the Motorhome Scratch

I was with some friends as they went to trade in their motorhome at a dealership. Everything seemed to go smoothly, and on the drive back, the husband sighed and commented that he was glad the dealer hadn't noticed a scratch on the motorhome's roof.

Sitting beside him, his wife reacted sharply, looking at him with shock and dismay.

"What scratch on the roof?" she demanded. She was taken aback because, until that moment, she'd been told there was no damage to the vehicle.

The husband hesitated, explaining that, some time back, he had accidentally scratched the top of the van while backing it up near a ladder.

Knowing his wife struggled with anxiety, he'd chosen to keep the information from her, hoping to spare her unnecessary worry.

He hadn't thought it was worth repairing—a minor scratch on a part of the motorhome hardly anyone would ever see.

But now, with the motorhome sold and out of their lives, he figured it was safe to mention. His wife felt betrayed, interpreting his decision as dishonesty. She was hurt and angry, feeling that he had lied to avoid trouble.

As their frustration simmered, I suggested a different perspective.

I shared with them the idea of *intent over deed.* I explained that, from what I could see, the husband's intention wasn't to deceive or belittle her feelings. Instead, his decision had been an act of love and concern.

Knowing her anxiety would be triggered by the damage, he had chosen to keep it to himself, sparing her from unnecessary stress and worry over something he couldn't change.

At that moment, it was a complex concept for her. But a few weeks later, we met again, and she thanked me. She'd had time to think about it, and with the initial anger gone, she saw her husband's actions in a new light.

Rather than trying to deceive her, he'd been acting from a place of care, hoping to shield her from distress over a minor issue that had no solution. His actions, she realised, had come from love, not deceit.

Seeing Intent Through the Lens of Empathy

This story captures the essence of looking beyond the deed to understand the intention. When someone makes a mistake or acts in ways that disappoint us, their intent often differs significantly from the impact.

They may have acted from a place of love, confusion, or a desire to protect us. By focusing on the intention, we can often move from frustration to empathy and understanding.

This approach is precious when dealing with situations involving complex struggles, like addiction or deeply ingrained habits. When people are wrestling with these issues, their actions may be driven by internal conflicts beyond their control, making it difficult for them to act as they—or we—might prefer.

By understanding that their actions might not align with their intentions, we can approach them with compassion without necessarily excusing harmful behaviour.

Choosing to See Beyond Actions

For example, someone might frequently seek reassurance or act overly concerned with how others see them. Though frustrating, this behaviour may sometimes stem from a deep-seated need for validation rooted in childhood or past experiences.

They may not even recognise how these patterns influence them. By considering this, we gain a clearer view of what's driving their actions.

We shift from reacting to observing when focusing on intentions rather than deeds. This doesn't mean we ignore hurtful actions, but it allows us to take a step back, considering the person's deeper motivations before we respond.

Responding with Empathy, Not Judgment

Responding with empathy means making a conscious effort to understand the entire picture before reacting. It's not about excusing hurtful actions but recognising the underlying struggle or motivation.

This mindset allows us to find compassion even in difficult moments. In doing so, we also find that our responses become more balanced and thoughtful, offering us peace in situations that might otherwise trigger anger or resentment.

Understanding the intent behind actions can also guide us in setting healthier boundaries. When we see someone's actions stem from pain or past wounds, we can respond with empathy while protecting ourselves.

Empathy doesn't mean tolerating harmful behaviours but creating space for understanding without compromising our well-being.

Reflection: Choosing Understanding Over Judgment

Life frequently presents situations where others' actions can cause hurt or confusion. When this happens, it's natural to feel defensive or frustrated.

However, by reflecting on the intention behind these actions, we can better understand the people around us.

1. **Recognising the Role of Intention**

Think of a recent time when someone's actions upset you. Reflect on what might have motivated their behaviour. Was it a genuine mistake, a habit, or a response driven by insecurity or anxiety?

Consider how viewing their intentions might shift your perspective.

2. **Using Empathy in Challenging Situations**

Empathy allows us to see actions in a new light. Recall a time when you encountered someone struggling with a personal issue, like addiction or stress.

Reflect on how recognising their struggle might help you approach similar situations with patience and understanding.

3. **Releasing Immediate Judgment**

It's easy to judge someone quickly, especially when we feel hurt. The next time you're frustrated by someone's behaviour, try pausing to ask yourself, "What might they be going through?"

This simple question can lead to a more thoughtful response.

4. **Setting Boundaries Mindfully**

Empathy doesn't mean accepting all behaviours. Reflect on a situation where you needed to set a boundary.

By approaching it with understanding, you may find a way to protect yourself while respecting the other person's struggles.

Moving Forward with a Balanced Perspective

When we focus on intent rather than deed, we open ourselves to a more compassionate view of others. Each interaction becomes an opportunity to see beyond behaviour and connect with the person behind it.

This approach fosters understanding and patience, bringing us closer to a life where empathy and kindness shape our responses.

In the story of the scratched motorhome, the wife's frustration eventually gave way to understanding. By recognising her husband's intent, she moved beyond the hurt to a place of acceptance and compassion.

This shift, though small, transformed their relationship, fostering a deeper connection and a renewed sense of trust.

Remember to look beyond the deed and consider the intent the next time someone's actions leave you feeling hurt or confused. In this way, we cultivate empathy for others and ourselves, embracing a more peaceful, understanding way of moving through the world.

Breaking Free from Self-Fulfilling Prophecies

Shaping a Future Beyond Expectations

In this chapter, let's explore the concept of self-fulfilling prophecies—the powerful, often subtle way our beliefs can shape our reality, sometimes to our detriment.

Consider the story of a woman who consults a tarot reader, who predicts she will meet a "tall, blonde-haired man" who is her true destiny. Although the woman is married, the prophecy begins to plant doubt in her mind.

As time passes, her belief in the reader's words

grows, undermining her marriage and leading her to seek someone who fits the description, turning the prophecy into reality.

This is how self-fulfilling prophecies work: We give them life by choosing to believe in and act on them, consciously or unconsciously. We begin creating them by expecting or even searching for specific outcomes.

The Power of Free Will

Our lives are not scripted by fate but are shaped by choices. Free will is a profound gift that allows us to steer our course regardless of predictions or outside influences. As we make our own decisions, we craft our unique journey, even if guidance from others suggests otherwise.

Predictions may suggest possible outcomes, but they're not definitive. At each moment, we have the power to redirect our path.

The crucial takeaway is this: just because someone predicts something doesn't mean you are bound to it. You can choose, question, or even dismiss any prophecy or advice. Trust your agency, and remember you create your reality through your choices.

Testing Prophecies Against Your Soul's Wisdom

So, how do you distinguish what aligns with your soul's path versus what may be external noise? As you connect more to your intuition, you will develop a stronger sense of what resonates with your soul's truth.

There will come a time when you no longer need to seek validation from external sources, like tarot readers or psychics, because you'll be tuned to the guidance of your inner wisdom.

Until then, seeking support and advice along the way is natural. But remember, you have the right to accept or reject any guidance. When someone offers a prediction or insight, could you take a moment to feel it out?

Does it resonate deeply? Does it align with your

sense of direction or cause discomfort or hesitation? If it feels discordant, let it go. Not every piece of advice is meant for you.

Trusting Your Soul's Guidance

Learning to trust your soul's guidance takes practice and patience. Your soul's wisdom surpasses any external opinion or prediction because it reflects your true self, purpose, and journey.

People may offer insights with the best of intentions, but remember that their perspective is influenced by their experiences, beliefs, and paths. Only you can fully understand your intentions and the direction of your soul.

When in doubt, always return to the quiet knowing within. Listen to your intuition; it's a powerful compass. Over time, you will learn to discern which advice is worth considering and which is best left behind. In this way, you keep your journey firmly in your own hands, guided by the wisdom that lies within.

Reflection: Navigating Predictions with Inner Wisdom

Self-fulfilling prophecies remind us that predictions do not hold power—it's the belief we invest in them that does. Free will is our most valuable asset, allowing us to shape our lives in ways that resonate with our soul's truth rather than external forecasts or expectations.

Reflecting on the nature of free will reminds us that predictions are possibilities, not certainties.

1. **Recognising When Beliefs Shape Reality**

Reflect on times when you've held a strong belief, whether positive or negative, that ultimately influenced your actions. Did it lead you closer to what you wanted, or did it hold you back?

Recognising how beliefs shape your reality can help you become more mindful of the influence of predictions and external opinions.

2. **Testing Outside Advice Against Inner Wisdom**

We often encounter advice that doesn't resonate, whether from friends, family, or spiritual guides. Reflect on when you received guidance that didn't sit right with you. How did you know it wasn't meant for you?

Trusting this inner dissonance can strengthen your ability to navigate future advice with confidence and clarity.

3. **Strengthening Intuitive Discernment**

As you build a relationship with your intuition, practice discerning whether information aligns with your inner truth. If you receive a suggestion or prediction, give yourself space to reflect on it. Does it align with your values and goals, or feel like a distraction?

Strengthening this discernment over time helps you navigate life with a more explicit purpose.

4. **Honouring Free Will**

Reflect on the power of free will in shaping your journey. Have you ever felt pressure to follow a path suggested by others, only to realise it wasn't suitable for you?

By honouring your choices, you can stay true to the life you're creating for yourself, guided by the unique wisdom of your soul.

5. **Building Self-Trust**

Predictions and prophecies can tempt us to seek answers outside ourselves, but proper guidance often comes from within. Reflect on moments when trusting yourself led to positive outcomes.

Each experience of listening to your inner guidance builds your self-trust, reminding you that the best compass is the one within.

Moving Forward with Confidence in Your Inner Guidance

This chapter encourages you to embrace your journey without being swayed by every prediction or opinion. Life is a path that we forge with our choices, guided by free will and inner wisdom.

By learning to filter external guidance through the lens of your soul's truth, you can create a life that feels authentic and aligned with who you are.

As you move forward, remember that you are the ultimate authority over your life's direction. Each decision shapes the life you are meant to live. Trust your inner compass, let go of predictions that don't resonate, and confidently create a life that reflects your most profound truths.

Beyond Filters: Embracing Truth's Complexity

Expanding Perception in a Multi-Faceted World

The future has fascinated humanity for centuries, and for a good reason, too. The idea of predicting or controlling what lies ahead is alluring.

But amid endless theories—some suggesting that time twists and bends beyond our perception, making it possible to jump to future points—there's one truth I feel deeply: we have free will. Every fibre of my being believes that while we can anticipate the future to some extent, it remains unwritten, shaped by our choices at each moment.

The Argument Against Predestination

The concept of causal determinism argues that if the future were fixed, accountability would vanish. Imagine a scenario where someone is destined to commit a crime, such as murder. If this act were predestined, they'd have no choice—no actual control over their actions.

However, free will implies that we can choose and hold responsibility for our actions. Each option, then, creates a ripple effect, altering the possible paths we take in life.

I firmly believe the future isn't prewritten. Instead, it unfolds based on our choices and information, like watching a branching path appear step by step. This perspective allows us to glimpse future outcomes without being bound to them.

A Story of Prediction

Once, while travelling with my friend Terry Smith, he shared an intriguing story. Terry had a vivid dream while in America, seeing himself go to Las Vegas, betting on a roulette number and winning twice on the same number in a row. Inspired by this vision,

Terry altered his plans, heading to Vegas to see if the dream held any truth. To his astonishment, the events unfolded exactly as he'd dreamed, and he walked away with a nice win.

This story might suggest that the future can be predicted. But I see it differently—Terry's dream influenced his decision to go to Vegas. By choosing to act on it, he turned it into a self-fulfilling prophecy. Had he ignored the dream, he likely wouldn't have ended up in Vegas.

The Power of Perspective

The following day, Terry and I were by the banks of Loch Lochy in Scotland. As we watched the water, two divers appeared, prepping for an underwater adventure. They mentioned that their air tanks would allow them to stay underwater for about 30 minutes before resurfacing.

We watched them disappear beneath the waves.

Later, a young couple settled at the water's edge, above where the divers had gone. I turned to Terry and remarked, "Here's a real-life example of how the future can be predicted with enough information."

Terry looked intrigued. "What do you mean?" he asked.

"We know the divers went under 20 minutes ago," I said, "and they'll need to resurface soon. The couple near the shore has no idea what's coming, but I bet they're about to get quite shocked when the divers pop up right before them."

Within moments, the divers resurfaced, sending the couple into startled surprise.

My prediction came true, not because the future was prewritten, but because we needed more information to see what was likely to happen—this moment reminded me of how perspective can shape our understanding of future possibilities without dictating them.

***The Source's* Perspective**

Imagine *the Source* as having a helicopter view of our lives, watching events unfold with far more insight than we could ever see on the ground. It can foresee specific outcomes based on trajectory and speed, like someone observing two cars headed towards an intersection.

While this view gives it insight, it doesn't force events to unfold a certain way. It observes, gently nudging, but the final choices remain ours.

From this elevated perspective, the future remains fluid. Free will is like an artist's brush, painting possibilities that shift and change with each decision we make.

Rather than seeing the future as set, *the Source* respects our autonomy, offering guidance without enforcing a fixed path.

Reflection: Embracing Free Will and the Power of Perspective

1. **The Dynamic Role of Free Will**

This chapter emphasises free will as a powerful tool for shaping our future, proving that our lives are not predestined but actively crafted by our decisions.

Reflect on past choices that have led to unexpected or transformative outcomes.

Recognising the impact of each decision, no matter how small, can bring new meaning to the power of free will in your life.

2. **Seeing Through the Lens of Perspective**

The examples in this chapter show how knowledge and awareness can shape our expectations about what's to come.

Think about situations where you've been able to anticipate an outcome based on your understanding of events.

This foresight empowers rather than restricts you, reinforcing that we aren't powerless bystanders.

3. **Guidance from a Higher Perspective**

Imagining *the Source* as a helicopter view of our lives can offer comfort, reminding us that guidance is available without stripping us of our autonomy.

Have you ever felt a subtle nudge or inner wisdom suggesting a specific choice?

Instead of feeling bound to a destiny, consider these insights as encouragement from a broader perspective rather than a directive.

4. **Balancing Prediction with Possibility**

Just as we could foresee specific outcomes for the divers and the couple by the shore, life presents moments that seem to follow predictable patterns. However, each pattern remains open to change, reinforcing that free will allows us to explore new directions.

Reflect on a time when you felt "locked" into a path yet made a choice that changed the trajectory. This realisation reminds you that the future is still yours to shape.

Exercises to Embrace Free Will in an Open Future

Exercise 1: Reflecting on Free Will and Choice

•Take a moment to write about when a decision

significantly changed your path.

Reflect on how that choice unfolded and consider what the alternative might have looked like.

•Consider your current decisions. Is there a choice you've been considering but hesitating to make?

Write down how choosing one way or another might shape your desired future, and make a decision with clarity and intention.

Exercise 2: Expanding Perspective

• Consider a current goal or challenge and list all the relevant factors affecting your decision-making.

Imagine taking a step back, much like a helicopter view, to see the situation from a broader perspective.

What new insights or possibilities emerge when you expand your view?

•Try to consider additional information or options you hadn't initially considered. This exercise can help you see new opportunities, much like how *the Source* world might offer gentle guidance.

Exercise 3: Embracing the Unknown with Curiosity

•Set aside five minutes daily to embrace uncertainty as a creative space. During this time, breathe deeply and mentally release the need to know exactly how things will turn out.

•Visualise yourself stepping into an unfolding journey, where each step is revealed in its own time.

This practice helps build trust in co-creating with free will, allowing the future to unfold without the pressure of needing complete control.

Moving Forward with Free Will and the Future

Rather than waiting passively for the future to arrive, this chapter invites you to see each moment as an opportunity to shape your path intentionally.

With free will, we possess an incredible tool for building a future aligned with our values, purpose, and inner guidance. As you move forward, remember that each choice carries power, offering you the freedom to evolve, adapt, and embrace life's unfolding possibilities.

With trust in your path and the guidance available,

you create a future that reflects your most authentic self, one intentional step at a time.

Part 5: Practical Wisdom for Living with Purpose

Spilt Milk and New Beginnings

A Practical Guide to Reflection and Renewal

Life is filled with unexpected setbacks, frustrations, and disappointments—those moments we might call "spilt milk." These are the times when things go awry, plans go sideways, and events beyond our control create frustration or regret.

It's tempting to hold onto anger or resentment, wondering why such things happen. But there is little point in lingering on these moments, as holding onto these emotions doesn't change the past or improve the future.

The following story illustrates the power of letting go and shows that what we learn from these moments is often more valuable than any attempt to reverse them.

The Tilted Window Lesson

When I set out to convert my Volkswagen T6 camper van, I enlisted the help of a friend to fit some of the windows. Fitting a window on a van involves cutting into the side panel—a process that leaves no room for error.

Once you cut that hole, it's permanent. We worked together on the first window, carefully measuring the placement. I showed him how I lined up the cut by measuring from the lower line of the van to ensure the window would sit level.

With the first window successfully fitted, I passed the reins to my friend, who felt confident about installing the second one. He approached the job with his measurement method, checking from top to bottom of the panel rather than from the van's base.

When he'd finished, we stepped back and realised the second window was slightly offset from the first.

Unless you looked closely, it wasn't obvious; however, with both of us having a hint of OCD, it was a detail that could nag at us.

My friend looked apologetic, expecting me to react with frustration or disappointment. After all, we could do nothing—the hole was cut, and the window was in.

"Don't worry about it. It's done," I said, shrugging it off. I could see he was baffled by my relaxed response.

"But... the windows don't line up," he said, clearly unsettled.

"Yep, but it's done and can't be fixed," I replied calmly. "It's just spilt milk, so let's put it down and move on."

He was still taken aback, but he absorbed the

lesson. There was no point in obsessing over the slight misalignment—what was done was done, and we couldn't change it. Life had already moved on, so why shouldn't we?

The Lesson Returns

A year later, my friend called to tell me a story of his own—a story that, in his words, could have sent him spiralling. He also lives in his van, and one morning, he accidentally reversed it into a container, causing damage down the rear corner.

His rear light was smashed, the paint was scraped, and the metal was dented.

Under normal circumstances, he admitted he would have been devastated, berating himself for days. He might have dwelt on his perceived carelessness, replaying the moment in his mind and turning the accident into a more significant burden.

But instead, he remembered the tilted window incident and the simple advice I'd given him: *It's just spilt milk.*

Instead of spiralling into frustration, he looked at the damage objectively. He gathered the pieces of the broken light, glued them back together, and temporarily reattached them until he could buy a replacement.

He took care of the exposed metal as best he could, touching up the paintwork, and ultimately decided there was nothing more to be done. So he let it go.

Later, he told me how liberating it was to approach the situation calmly and that he probably would have reacted very differently if it hadn't been for the tilted window lesson. Instead, he was able to accept the setback, make the best of it, and move on.

The Nature of Reality: Free Will and Randomness

Like many of life's setbacks, this story reminds us that not everything is within our control. Life is governed by natural laws and our free will rather than by *the Source* micromanaging every little detail.

The universe operates within a complex network of interconnections, but that doesn't mean every positive or negative incident is orchestrated. Like the leaves on a tree, we are nourished and supported by *the Source*.

Yet, even as we're connected to this energy, we're subject to life's elements—the wind, the rain, the unexpected bumps along the way.

Like illness, accidents, or a slightly misaligned window, setbacks are natural parts of life's journey. They don't need to be dissected or obsessed over; they must be accepted, handled, and released.

Embracing "Spilt Milk" Moments

When faced with life's inevitable "spilt milk" moments, consider the following approach:

1. **Assess the Situation**:

Determine if there's anything you can do immediately. If so, take that action without delay.

If it's fixing a minor error, mending a broken item,

or handling a misunderstanding, act on it promptly.

2. **Plan for the Future**:
If something can be addressed later, set a specific time and place. Please make a note, set a reminder, and shift your focus to the present until it's time to revisit the issue.

3. **Let Go If Necessary**:
For situations beyond your control, like a permanent dent or a tilted window, acknowledge the event, accept that it's part of your path, and let it go. Energy wasted on resentment or regret only serves to hold you back.

Reflection and Letting Go

The lesson of the tilted window and the dented van reminds us that big or small setbacks don't need to become burdens. We can choose to handle them, learn from them, and move on without allowing them to overshadow our peace.

By letting go of "spilt milk," we shift our focus from regret to progress, making room for what lies ahead.

Whether it's a tilted window or a damaged bumper, the event itself doesn't define us—our ability to release it does.

Moving Forward with Peace

In life, setbacks will always appear. Some, like a slight misalignment or a fender bender, are minor. Others might feel more profound. But how we respond determines our journey.

By focusing on what we can control, releasing what we can't, and viewing each setback as an opportunity to practice resilience, we build the strength to face each new challenge calmly and clearly.

The next time something doesn't go as planned, remember to *handle what you can, let go of what you can't and keep moving forward.*

Life isn't about avoiding the spilt milk; it's about knowing when to clean up and when to let it be simple. Through this mindset, we free ourselves to enjoy each new step.

The Indirect Path

Navigating Life's Surprising Turns

One phrase has become my mantra for life's unpredictable journey: "A to B via C." It captures the reality that, aiming to get from point A (where we are) to point B (where we want to be), we're often detoured to point C, a place we never expected to go.

Life rarely leads us down a straight path. Instead, we find ourselves meandering through twists and turns that, while frustrating at the moment, are often the experiences we need to grow.

The Detours That Shape Us

I've often set out confidently toward point B throughout my life, only to end up at an unexpected point C. Early in my career, I had clear goals, only to be offered roles that felt utterly off-track. What seemed irrelevant at the time turned out to be invaluable.

These "detours" built skills and resilience, making me better prepared for the ultimate roles I aimed for. Much like constructing a house requires building a solid foundation, sometimes point C is the groundwork for the goals at point B.

Looking back, I realise those detours were not distractions; they were part of the journey I couldn't skip. They equipped me with insights and abilities essential for my final destination. Without those moments at point C, I wouldn't have been able to thrive once I reached point B.

The Importance of Point C

Point C is not a pointless pit stop; it's where

transformation happens. This is where we gather the skills, knowledge, and perspective to appreciate and fully navigate point B. Challenges, setbacks, or redirections often serve as tests or training, preparing us for the next chapter.

Point C is where we gain the tools to succeed once we arrive at our destination.

Imagine point B as the peak of a mountain. Reaching the summit requires building endurance and strength along the way. Without these tests, we'd struggle at higher altitudes. Similarly, point C is where we collect the "gear" we need to face the summit.

Embrace the Journey Through C

Stuck at point C, it can feel like we've been thrown off course. Instead of resisting, we can embrace the detour, understanding it as an essential part of the journey. Ask yourself, "What am I learning here?

How can this experience help me in the future?" With time, these answers often become apparent.

For example, if you're facing career setbacks, maybe point C teaches you perseverance or indicates a new direction. If you're dealing with personal hardship, perhaps point C is helping you build empathy or self-awareness.

The qualities we develop through life's detours become essential assets later on.

An Analogy: The Scenic Route

Imagine you're on a road trip, planning to take the fastest route from A to B. A roadblock suddenly forces you onto an unplanned detour. At first, you're frustrated.

But as you continue, you find yourself driving through beautiful landscapes, stopping at a small café for incredible coffee, and meeting people who leave a lasting impression.

When you finally reach your destination, you realise the detour enriched the trip.

Had you taken the direct route, you would have missed these experiences. In life, point C is that scenic route. It's not the most efficient path, but it often holds the most growth and insight.

The Detours Are the Journey

Ultimately, life isn't about a quick arrival at point B but the journey itself. The detours and delays, while inconvenient, add layers of experience, growth, and resilience that shape who we are.

The next time you find yourself at an unexpected point C, remember that it's part of the plan—even if you can't see it yet. Embrace the scenic route, trust the process, and let the journey unfold.

Reflection: Embracing the Lessons of Point C

The road from A to B is rarely straight. Instead, life often leads us through unexpected detours—points C, D, and beyond—that enrich our journey.

At these unplanned stops, we find experiences and lessons that we'll later recognise as essential to our growth.

1. **Seeing Point C as Preparation, Not a Setback**

Reflect on moments when life didn't go as planned. Maybe you faced a job change, an unplanned move, or a personal setback.

Consider how these detours prepared you for future challenges. When we view C as a part of the journey rather than a diversion, finding meaning in these experiences becomes easier.

2. **Trusting in Life's Scenic Routes**

Detours often lead us through unexpected beauty. Consider when an unplanned route brought new friendships, insights, or opportunities.

Remembering the scenic moments in life's detours helps us embrace the twists and turns with greater trust, knowing that these side routes are often where we find true richness.

3. **Recognising Growth Along the Way**

The unplanned stops on our journey often reveal

what we're capable of.

Reflect on challenges that forced you to develop resilience, empathy, or patience. By recognising these qualities, we see how point C, rather than delaying us, may have strengthened us for the path ahead.

4. **Letting Go of Frustration at Point C**

Life's detours can feel disheartening, but frustration often arises from resisting the journey. Consider how letting go of rigid timelines or expectations might ease the trip.

Embracing the path, even when it goes through unexpected points, can make us more open to the lessons and gifts along the way.

Moving Forward with Trust in the Journey

Life is not a straight path from A to B, and the detours are often where we find the most growth and meaning.

Each time we land at point C, we can collect new insights and strengths to support us later. Embrace these moments, knowing they're part of the journey you were meant to take.

Rather than focusing solely on the destination, appreciate each step of the journey. Trust in the detours, embrace the scenic routes and recognise that point C is not a distraction but an integral part of the adventure.

With each turn, you become more prepared for what lies ahead, carrying the wisdom and resilience gained from every step.

The Transformative Power of Gratitude

Shifting Your Mindset to Embrace Life's Gifts

It's too easy to fall into a negative mindset daily, dwelling on minor frustrations or disappointments. You might catch yourself spiralling into grey thoughts or feeling gloomy about things that aren't as planned.

The frustration of being cut off in traffic ignites an immediate desire for karmic justice. Or it might be something more profound, like feeling disheartened by setbacks and wondering if things will ever change.

These thought loops can make it feel as if there's no escape.

But there is a way out, and it's simple yet powerful: gratitude.

Gratitude can profoundly shift your mindset. Here's why: just as darkness cannot remain in the presence of light, negative emotions struggle to coexist with genuine thankfulness.

You can't hold onto anger or frustration while genuinely focusing on something you're grateful for. The two can't occupy the same space.

A Simple Method for Shifting Your Mindset with Gratitude

The next time you find yourself falling into negativity, try this easy method to realign your focus:

1. Recognise the Negative Thought

Awareness is the first step. Pause for a moment

and acknowledge what's happening. Notice if you're ruminating over something frustrating or disappointing.

Take a deep breath and let yourself step back from the thought spiral.

2. Shift to Gratitude

Replace the negative thought with something you are genuinely grateful for, big or small. This might include:

•The love of someone who cares for you.

Focus on that bond and feel the warmth of their support.

•Your health and abilities.

Even if life has challenges, there's something to appreciate about your body or mind.

•A pet who brings you joy.

Please think of the comfort and happiness they add to your life.

•A holiday memory or exciting plans.

Visualise a peaceful or adventurous place that lifts your spirits.

•Simply waking up today.

The new day itself is a chance for fresh experiences and moments.

3. Build Your Gratitude List

Creating a ready-made list of things you're grateful for can be incredibly helpful.

Write down ten things that spark gratitude—big or small. These don't have to be profound; even small joys can have a powerful impact. Keep this list close and refer to it whenever negativity creeps in.

4. Engage Your Emotions

As you think of these things, allow yourself to feel gratitude. Rather than quickly moving through each item, let yourself experience the associated emotions.

This isn't about simply listing things off but engaging deeply with feelings of appreciation.

The Science Behind Gratitude

Research has shown that gratitude has measurable effects on our well-being. Practising gratitude can reduce stress, boost mood, and improve physical health.

When you actively focus on things you're thankful for, your brain adjusts, helping you approach life with a brighter, healthier perspective.

The next time you're slipping into negativity, try reaching for gratitude. It's a powerful tool, accessible at any moment, that can help guide your mind back to peace.

You may not be able to control every situation, but you can control how you perceive it. Through gratitude, you invite positivity and resilience into your life.

Take a moment to start your gratitude list now.

Please write down the things that bring you joy, feel them deeply, and keep this list close.

When negativity arises, let gratitude be your guiding light.

Reflection: Embracing Gratitude to Transform Your Mindset

1. **Recognising Negative Patterns**

Life brings many minor frustrations that can quickly pull us into negative cycles. Reflect on times when you've found yourself spiralling in frustration.

Recognising these patterns is the first step towards breaking free and redirecting your focus.

2. **The Power of Gratitude to Shift Perspective**

Gratitude can bring peace by drawing your attention to what's going right. Recall a recent moment when focusing on something positive, even briefly, helped lift your mood.

This memory can remind you of the impact of

gratitude and encourage you to practise it in times of need.

3. **Using a Personal Gratitude List**

Use the personal gratitude list you made earlier.

4. **Engaging Fully with Gratitude**

Engage deeply with your gratitude, allowing yourself to truly appreciate each moment or person.

Reflect on how immersing yourself in this practice can transform gratitude from a fleeting thought to a grounding force.

5. **The Science of Gratitude**

Knowing gratitude has real effects can motivate you to practice it regularly.

Reflect on how gratitude has improved your mood or resilience, helping you navigate life's challenges calmly and optimistically.

Exercises: Practising Gratitude Daily

Exercise 1: A Moment of Gratitude

•Set aside five minutes each morning to think of three things you're grateful for. This can be as simple as a warm cup of tea, a restful night's sleep, or the people in your life.

Write them down, and try to think of new things each morning.

Exercise 2: Gratitude in the Face of Negativity

•The next time you slip into a negative thought spiral, pause. Take three deep breaths and recall a moment or person you're grateful for.

Focus on the feelings this memory brings, allowing gratitude to replace the negative thoughts.

Exercise 3: Building a Gratitude Journal

•Start a gratitude journal and aim to write in it at least three times a week. Include both big things and small daily joys.

By regularly writing down your blessings, you train your mind to focus more on the positives in your life.

Exercise 4: A Gratitude Jar

•Place a jar somewhere visible and add a note each day with something you're grateful for. Over time, this jar will fill with reminders of life's blessings.

Pull out a few notes to lift your spirits when you're feeling low.

Exercise 5: Sharing Gratitude

•Think of someone who has positively impacted your life and tell them in person or by writing them a note.

Sharing gratitude deepens your connection with them and reinforces your focus on the positives.

Moving Forward: Choosing Gratitude as a Guiding Light

This chapter invites you to use gratitude as a foundation for resilience and positivity. By focusing on gratitude, you're not ignoring challenges but creating a balance, allowing life's small blessings to keep you grounded.

Let gratitude become a daily practice, a guiding light that helps you navigate challenges with grace.

Whenever you feel negativity rising, please take a deep breath, reach for gratitude, and let it fill your mind. Through this practice, you're shifting your perspective and inviting a brighter, more resilient self to emerge.

Gratitude is your steady compass—embrace it, let it guide you, and allow it to transform your mindset.

Creating Ripples of Kindness

Inspiring Positive Change One Act at a Time

The Source often works through us in everyday acts—nudging us to perform seemingly random gestures that, in reality, spark the coincidences that shape others' lives.

These aren't grand miracles that defy logic but rather those small, spontaneous moments where we're inspired to act—perhaps without fully understanding why at the time.

Many people, myself included, have consciously

given *the Source* permission to use us as channels for these acts. By tuning into these gentle prompts—whether it's a sudden urge to help someone or a feeling to take a different route home—we open ourselves to participate in something meaningful.

Though these small acts may feel insignificant, they often become part of something much larger than we'd ever imagined.

It could be something as simple as letting someone merge in front of you in traffic or striking up an unexpected conversation with someone in a supermarket queue.

These actions seem trivial on their own, but when we look back, we can often see how they created ripples that touched lives far beyond what we'd anticipated.

Random Acts of Kindness and Paying It Forward

Let's discuss two key ideas: random acts of kindness

and paying it forward.

Imagine a world where everyone is committed to a tiny act of kindness daily. What if kindness became the automatic, instinctual choice in our interactions with others?

A smile at a stranger, holding a door open, giving up your seat on the bus—small gestures, yes, but imagine their potential impact if everyone did them.

If we paused before every interaction to ask ourselves, *"What would kindness do here?"* How would our actions change? Imagine if we all helped those struggling or accepted help ourselves with gratitude.

How different would our world look if kindness were the rule, not the exception?

When we make these spontaneous gestures a daily practice, no matter how small, *the Source* works through us, spreading ripples of kindness and goodwill. The beauty of these acts lies not in their size but in their sincerity, freely given and offered without expecting anything in return.

The second idea is *Paying It Forward.* When we do something kind for someone, they often want to repay the favour.

And while it's lovely to feel appreciated, there's an even more significant impact when we invite people to "pay it forward" instead of simply returning the kindness to us. When someone offers to repay me, I often ask them to pass it on—"do something kind for someone else."

Doing this creates a chain of kindness, spreading far and wide.

If each of us paid it forward just 10% of the time, the ripple effect of kindness would spread globally, impacting countless lives. Imagine a world where children are raised with this mindset—to spread kindness beyond themselves.

We could create a society where acts of generosity flow from one person to another, creating an unbroken chain of goodwill.

Each time someone pays it forward, they carry the

spirit of kindness into their day. Your original act becomes a spark, setting off a chain reaction that could change lives in ways you may never see.

You begin a positive chain that extends well beyond your initial gesture by igniting this flame of kindness.

Reflection: Becoming a Channel for Kindness

1. **Embracing Subtle Nudges**

The Source often communicates through subtle nudges, prompting us to act without knowing why.

Reflect on a time when you felt urged to help or connect unexpectedly. What happened as a result? Consider how noticing these nudges might make a difference in your life and the lives around you.

2. **Cultivating Everyday Kindness**

Imagine kindness as second nature, as automatic as breathing.

Reflect on small gestures—like a smile, a helping hand, or giving up your place in a queue—that uplift others. How would a world where everyone practised such kindness daily change not only your day but your community's energy?

3. **The Ripple Effect of Kindness**

Kindness often creates ripples beyond what we can see. Think about when someone's kindness left a lasting impression on you. How did it shape your actions or attitude?

Imagine being *the Source* of such a ripple for others, knowing that each act of kindness could extend far beyond you.

4. **Paying It Forward**

Paying it forward allows kindness to grow beyond a single moment, creating a chain of goodwill.

Consider ways to encourage others to pass kindness on instead of reciprocating directly. How might this make a collective ripple of kindness, reaching others in ways you'll never see firsthand?

5. **Living as a Vessel for *the Source***

When we act as vessels for kindness, we align ourselves more closely with *the Source*.

Reflect on a time you worked as a vessel for good, even without understanding the whole reason behind it. How could seeing yourself as a channel for kindness reshape your approach to daily interactions?

6. **Seeing the Bigger Picture**

Looking back, we often see how seemingly small actions contribute to a larger purpose.

Reflect on your journey with kindness. What patterns or connections reveal themselves? How can remembering these "dots" help you trust the value of small, everyday kindnesses moving forward?

Exercise: Sparking Your Chain Reaction

Commit to performing one spontaneous act of kindness each day for a week. Whether big or small, let it be something that feels genuine and unplanned.

After each act, if the recipient offers you a reward, ask them to "pay it forward."

At the end of the week, take a moment to reflect on how these simple actions impacted your sense of connection, gratitude, and positivity. You may never know the total reach of your kindness, but understand that every act you perform links to an ongoing chain of goodwill.

Use these reflections and exercises to deepen your purpose in practising kindness. When we act from a place of sincerity, we let *the Source* flow through us, turning each moment into part of a greater force for good.

Each small act we perform becomes part of a more significant wave of positivity, extending beyond what we may ever see, leaving the world a little better with each gesture.

Win When Nobody Else Loses

Fostering Collaborative Success for All

Many dream of winning the lottery, visualising a massive life change that seems within reach if the stars align. But before getting too caught up in the allure of this possibility, consider the implications. Winning a lottery isn't relatively as straightforward as it seems when viewed through the lens of spiritual principles.

The universe, or *the Source*, doesn't work by placing one person's wishes over another's, especially not for something as arbitrary as lottery winnings. Every ticket buyer hopes for success, so if *the Source* were to favour your ticket above another, it would bypass the free will and intentions of countless others.

The Source operates on a principle of balance, avoiding "wins" that come at the expense of others. Instead, its energy flows toward uplifting and connecting, creating outcomes where everyone benefits.

This universal approach aligns with the principles of a particular group of people, often called conduits, lightworkers, or rainbow warriors.

These individuals have chosen to serve as channels for positive energy, using the resources that flow to them—financial, emotional, or spiritual—to benefit others in need.

Through them, kindness becomes a currency, creating wins that lift others without any losses.

Being a Conduit for *the Source*

In my life, I've had moments where I've found

myself guided to buy something expensive, only to feel the urge to pass it on to someone else. Initially, this felt counterintuitive.

But when I noticed that giving often led to an unexpected flow of new clients or resources, I realised I was simply a channel, allowing resources to pass through me to others. *The Source* seems to replenish what we give away, ensuring that we're sustained while helping others.

Take, for example, a time I felt compelled to buy a camera. I didn't know why I needed it, but the pull was undeniable. A few weeks later, a friend mentioned how much he wanted that specific camera model for his photography work. It became clear: I wasn't meant to keep it.

By gifting it to him, I acted in a flow of kindness and support that exceeded my needs. Soon after, my business income rose, a return that mirrored the value of my gift.

These moments demonstrate how *the Source* balances the exchange. Whenever we become a channel, passing on resources to others, we play a role in a much larger picture that honours everyone's intentions and uplifts the whole.

I have experienced many instances where we were moved to help those in need—buying a washing machine for a single mother, covering unexpected medical expenses for a friend, and more.

Through each act, I saw how generosity created abundance for everyone involved.

The Ripple Effect of Kindness

Acts of kindness extend beyond the moment, creating a ripple effect that continues influencing lives. When you give without expecting anything in return, you shift the recipient's life and your own.

This isn't about earning material rewards but creating a balance where resources flow where they are most needed. It's a win-win that leaves no one diminished.

So, the next time you feel a strong urge to share, even if it seems random, trust that *the Source* may guide you to be part of something bigger. *The Source* ensures that those who allow themselves to be conduits of kindness receive support in return, balancing the flow of giving and receiving.

This creates a cycle of abundance where everyone can win without anyone else having to lose.

Reflection: Being a Conduit for Positive Energy

This chapter encourages us to see abundance as more significant than individual gain. Instead of focusing on what we can accumulate, it asks us to consider how we can share and support others.

When we align ourselves with this flow, our lives shift from personal gain to collective support, creating meaningful wins that don't require anyone else's loss.

When we act as conduits for kindness, we often see that the energy we share returns to us, allowing us to continue the cycle. This balance brings about unexpected blessings and meets needs on all sides.

By focusing on what we can give, we find that abundance becomes a natural part of our experience, arising from genuine generosity and shared goodwill.

Moving Forward as a Conduit of Kindness

Allowing ourselves to be conduits requires trust but opens us to a greater purpose. When guided to help others, we become part of a more significant flow that fosters abundance and peace, creating opportunities for everyone to win in a way that transcends individual desires.

As we act on these nudges, we strengthen a world where success and kindness multiply, spreading balance and positivity for all involved.

Part 6: Tools for Reflection and Growth

The Weekly Compass

Weekly Reflections for Growth and Alignment

One of the most impactful practices for personal growth and life planning is the habit of weekly reflection and goal setting. This practice helps you assess where you are, recalibrate your focus, and intentionally choose your path forward.

I first learned the power of this habit from working under Andrew Evans, who used a weekly check-in that asked three simple but profound questions:

- Where am I?
- Where do I want to be?
- How am I going to get there?

These questions became the foundation of our progress, and I've since integrated them into my personal and spiritual practice.

I encourage you to make this a regular ritual, helping you reflect on your journey and align with your goals.

Step 1: Where Am I?

Begin by looking back at the past week. The goal isn't to judge yourself harshly but to honestly assess where you are in your journey.

Reflect on the goals you've set, the experiences you hoped to manifest, and any progress you've made. Ask yourself:

•How much progress did I make this past week?

•What accomplishments, even small ones, am I proud of?

•Did I notice any opportunities or coincidences that helped me?

•What setbacks or challenges did I face, and what lessons did they offer?

Even if progress is small, it's meaningful. A journal or notebook can be invaluable here, allowing you to jot down your weekly thoughts. Over time, this record becomes a powerful reminder of your journey and growth.

Pro Tip: Approach this reflection with curiosity rather than criticism. Progress often happens in incremental steps rather than grand leaps.

Step 2: Where Do I Want to Be?

Once you have a clear view of where you are, focus on where you want to go. This is your chance to reconnect with your vision and set specific goals. Remember that the future is shaped by the energy you bring to it. Reflect on:

•What are the goals or experiences I want to attract this week?

•Which areas of my life need more attention or care?

•Is there something I need to adjust or try differently?

Clarity is key. If you desire abundance, specify what that means—financial security, fulfilling relationships, or emotional well-being.

The clearer you are, the more aligned your energy becomes, making it easier for you (and *the Source*) to move toward those experiences.

Pro Tip: Focus on realistic, attainable goals. Long-term dreams are essential; weekly goals should be achievable and harmonised with your larger vision. Let the process unfold step-by-step.

Step 3: How Am I Going to Get There?

Now that you know where you are and where you want to go, it's time to plan your next steps.

Consider the specific actions you can take in the coming week to bring you closer to your goals. Some weeks, the steps will be clear; other times, you may not see an immediate path forward, and that's okay.

If the way forward isn't apparent, embrace a mindset of openness.

Commit to staying aware of opportunities and coincidences, allowing *the Source* to work in the background to create pathways you may not yet see. Some examples of actions include:

•Dedicate time each day to meditate or visualise your desired outcomes.

•Stay mindful of intuitive nudges—those moments when you feel inspired to reach out, take a different route, or try something new.

•Consistently work on a project, trusting that each effort is progress.

Pro Tip: If you don't know the next step, set an intention to remain open.

Trust that *the Source* always aligns circumstances

to support you, even if the path isn't immediately apparent.

Make It a Weekly Ritual

To fully embrace this practice, set aside a specific time each week. Pick a day to dedicate an hour to this reflection, on Sunday evening or Monday morning. In this uninterrupted space, follow the three steps:

1. **Where am I?** – Reflect on your progress.
2. **Where do I want to be?** – Set intentions for the upcoming week.
3. **How am I going to get there?** – Plan your action steps or commit to being open.

Turn this practice into a ritual. Creating this weekly routine invites *the Source* to support you and open yourself to emerging opportunities.

Writing your reflections and plans makes the experience more tangible, helping you stay accountable for your intentions.

Reflection: Staying Intentional on Your Journey

This chapter introduces a simple yet powerful way to cultivate focus and alignment. By regularly asking yourself, *Where am I? Where do I want to be? How am I going to get there?* You gain clarity and direction, building momentum toward your goals one week at a time.

This practice lets you see your journey as a series of conscious choices and actions, ensuring you stay connected to your deeper intentions.

1. The Power of Reflection in Growth

Weekly reflection gives you a clear view of your progress, helping you recognise each step forward. Think of a recent achievement or lesson that has shaped your growth, no matter how small.

Regularly revisiting your progress builds confidence and reminds you that growth is happening, even subtly.

2. Defining Your Vision with Precision

Clarity is essential for bringing your goals into reality. When setting your intentions for the coming week, focus on specific experiences or goals. Ask yourself: What would truly fulfil me this week?

Embrace meaningful goals, whether big or small, and allow them to guide your actions.

3. Embracing Flexibility in Your Plans

Only some steps will be clear; sometimes, the way forward requires flexibility. When faced with uncertainty, consider how staying open and receptive can invite new opportunities.

Trust that *the Source* works alongside you, creating possibilities that may surprise you.

4. Aligning Intentions with Weekly Action

Your intentions are powerful, but they become transformative when paired with action. As you plan your next steps, consider how small actions can have a cumulative impact.

This weekly practice builds a bridge between your goals and reality, creating momentum that brings your vision to life over time.

Moving Forward with Clarity and Purpose

This weekly practice is more than just a planning tool; it's a way to live intentionally, staying connected to what truly matters. You align your life with your highest purpose by reflecting on where you are, defining where you want to be, and creating action steps.

This journey isn't just about reaching a destination—it's about experiencing growth, learning from challenges, and celebrating each small success.

Let this practice become a source of strength, guiding you with clarity and purpose. Week by week, as you build this habit, you'll see how each reflection brings you closer to the experiences and life you desire.

Trust the process, stay open to possibilities, and

confidently move forward. The path to your dreams unfolds step by step, shaped by your intentions and guided by *the Source.*

A Guide to Daily, Weekly, and Monthly Reflection

Creating a Personal Practice to Align, Reflect, and Grow

Creating a personal, structured reflection practice can be life-changing. To make it easy to integrate, let's break down each step into a daily, weekly, and monthly routine. By the end of each week, month, and year, you'll be able to look back and see your progress and growth.

This section will walk you through setting up a reflection and goal-setting routine, step by step, so you always have the tools you need to stay aligned with your path.

Step 1: Setting Up Your Reflection Practice

What You'll Need:

1. **An A5-sized daily planner or diary**: Choose one with a page dedicated to each day. This will become your "Reflection Diary."
2. **This book**: Keep it with you as a guide, inspiration, and reminder of the bigger picture as you go about your daily practices.

When to Reflect:

1. **Set a specific time each day** for this practice—whether in the morning to set intentions or in the evening to reflect on the day. Ideally, find a quiet, comfortable space to focus without interruptions.

2. **Carry your Reflection Diary with you throughout the day** so you can note down any insights, feelings, or ideas as they come to you. You'll

find that reflection becomes easier as you integrate it into your routine.

Section 1: Daily Practices

Daily reflections are short, focusing exercises that help you stay aligned with your intentions. Aim to spend just 5–10 minutes a day on these entries.

1.1 Morning Intention Setting

•**Goal:** Start each day with a clear intention.

•**How-To:** Open your Reflection Diary each morning. Write down today's date and then set a simple intention by completing this sentence: "Today, I intend to..."

•**Example Entry:**

•**Date:** October 22, 2024

•**Today's Intention:** "I intend to focus on kindness in all my interactions and remain open to new opportunities."

•**Pro Tip:** Visualise yourself embodying this intention throughout the day. Picture small moments where kindness could guide your actions.

1.2 Noticing Opportunities

•**Goal:** Stay open to positive opportunities or moments of Intuition.

•**How-To:** During the day, jot down any coincidences or "nudges" you experience during the day. These might be encounters, insights, or signs that align with your intentions.

•**Example Entry:**

•**Opportunity Noticed:** "Ran into an old friend who invited me to an event that aligns with my career goals. Felt like a nudge from *the Source* to explore new connections."

•**Pro Tip:** If nothing comes up, don't worry. Note, "No specific opportunities noticed today," and be open for the next day.

1.3 Evening Reflection and Gratitude

•**Goal:** Reflect on the day and end with gratitude.

•**How-To:** Each evening, return to your Reflection Diary. Write down answers to the following:

1. **What went well today?**
2. **What did I learn?**
3. **What am I grateful for?** (List three things)

•**Example Entry:**

•**Today's Wins:** "I stayed calm during a challenging meeting and focused on solutions."

•**Lesson Learned:** "Patience can lead to better outcomes. I don't always need to react immediately."

•**Gratitude:**

1. "My supportive partner"
2. "A warm cup of tea in the morning"
3. "The unexpected encouragement from a colleague"

Section 2: Weekly Practices

Weekly practices help you check in on your progress, identify areas for growth, and set specific goals for the upcoming week. Schedule a consistent time each week (perhaps Sunday evening or Monday morning) to dedicate 20–30 minutes to this review.

2.1 Weekly Reflection: Where Am I?

•**Goal:** Review your week honestly.
•**How-To:** Answer these questions in your diary:

1. **What progress did I make this week?**
2. **What challenges did I face?**
3. **What opportunities or "signs" did I notice?**

•**Example Entry:**

•**Progress Made:** "Completed my work project ahead of time and had time to help a friend in need."

•**Challenges Faced:** "Felt stressed mid-week. Realised I need to take breaks."

•**Opportunities Noticed:** "Spontaneously invited to join a community group I've been interested in."

2.2 Goal Setting: Where Do I Want to Be?

•**Goal:** Set intentions for the upcoming week.

•**How-To:** Write down specific, achievable goals based on your review. Define clear actions for each goal.

•**Example Entry:**

•**Goal:** "Prioritise self-care to reduce stress."

•**Action Steps:**

•Take a 10-minute walk every morning.

•Dedicate 30 minutes to read before bed.

2.3 Letting Go Exercise

•**Goal:** Release any lingering frustrations or "spilt milk" moments.

•**How-To:** Write down anything from the week you want to let go of. Imagine letting it go and then moving on.

•Example Entry:

•Letting Go: "I'm releasing the stress I felt from a disagreement at work. I choose to learn from it and move forward."

Section 3: Monthly Practices

Monthly reflections deepen your progress and allow you to set meaningful goals that align with your soul's desires. This exercise may take 30–60 minutes, so find a quiet moment at the end of each month.

3.1 Monthly Review: Summing Up and Planning Ahead

•Goal: Look back on the month to recognise growth and set meaningful intentions for the next month.

•How-To: Answer these questions:

1. **What were my most meaningful experiences this month?**
2. **What did I learn from the challenges I faced?**

3. **What areas of my life need more attention or change?**

•Example Entry:

•Meaningful Experiences: "Developing a closer bond with my sibling, achieving a work milestone."

•Lessons Learned: "Patience and communication are key."

•Areas to Improve: "Focus on self-care and balance in my schedule."

3.2 Visualising Next Steps

•Goal: Set a vision for the next month.

• **How:** Spend a few moments visualising your ideal outcomes for the month ahead. Write down specific intentions or goals.

•Example Entry:

•Vision for the Month: "This month, I envision finding more balance and staying connected with loved ones."

•Intentions:

•"Dedicate one day each week to rest and self-care."

•"Reach out to a different friend or family member weekly."

3.3 Deepening Intuition

•Goal: Connect more deeply with your soul's desires.

• **How:** Sit quietly, close your eyes, and reflect on whether your goals align with your true self. Ask yourself, "Am I following my intuition or being influenced by outside pressures?"

•Example Entry:

•Soul Check-In: "I need to spend more time on creative pursuits. I'll set aside 20 minutes daily for writing, drawing, or another creative activity."

Bringing It All Together

Carrying your **Reflection Diary**, and this book will give you your roadmap for growth. These daily, weekly, and monthly exercises will guide you, helping you stay in tune with *the Source* and your soul's desires.

Remember, this is not about perfection but progress and staying connected to what truly matters to you.

Make this practice your own, adding thoughts, doodles, or anything else that reflects your journey. With each Entry, you're creating a personal record of transformation, one day at a time. Enjoy the journey!

Part 7: Final Thoughts and Community

Expanding Beyond Filters

Understanding and Embracing Broader Perspectives

Introduction: Understanding Our Perception of Truth

As human beings, our understanding of reality is inherently filtered. These filters are shaped by our experiences, beliefs, and the unique lenses through which we view the world.

Often, we interpret situations, people, and events based on what we already know, making it easy to overlook other perspectives or more profound truths.

The Source invites us to look beyond these filters,

urging us to embrace a more expansive view of reality and truth. This journey requires us to acknowledge our limitations, question our assumptions, and be willing to see the world—and ourselves—with greater clarity.

The Nature of Filters

From an early age, we develop filters to interpret the world. Our upbringing, culture, past experiences, and even societal expectations shape these filters. They act like tinted lenses, colouring everything we see and understand.

While filters can help process the vast amount of information around us, they can also lead us to interpret reality in limited or biased ways.

For example, if we believe that "success means financial wealth," we might only recognise specific achievements as valuable, overlooking accomplishments that don't fit this narrow definition.

In doing so, we miss out on broader interpretations of success that could be meaningful.

Seeing beyond these filters doesn't mean disregarding everything we've learned; it means recognising that our current perspective is only one among many. By becoming aware of our filters, we can see the world more openly and rationally.

The Role of the Source in Expanding Our Perception

The Source allows us to step back and view the bigger picture. We can see beyond our own perspective's limitations through reflection and openness to guidance. This guidance from *the Source* often comes as a gentle reminder—a nudge to question our assumptions or to look deeper when something feels unclear.

When we align with *the Source*, we start to see life's complexities not as obstacles but as layers of truth. The events we encounter, the people we meet, and our choices all carry meaning beyond what we immediately perceive.

In allowing ourselves to be guided by *the Source*, we're invited to explore these layers and embrace the fullness of reality beyond our initial filters.

Truth as a Multifaceted Concept

Truth is only sometimes a straightforward path. It often has multiple facets, and what feels true in one moment or context may look different from another angle. Recognising this complexity is critical to living in alignment with *the Source*, which encourages us to remain open to multiple truths and perspectives.

Consider an example where two people view the same event but interpret it differently. For one, the event might represent a challenge, while for the other, it's an opportunity. Neither perspective is "wrong"—people interpret the event based on their unique experiences.

This multiplicity doesn't diminish the event's reality but enriches our understanding.

Learning to see truth as layered teaches us empathy

for other perspectives and a more profound respect for the diversity of human experience. *The Source* reminds us that truth often transcends a single perspective, inviting us to consider how reality can be understood.

Embracing Uncertainty as Part of the Truth

We must also embrace uncertainty in seeking a more comprehensive view of truth. Human nature often gravitates toward definitive answers, yet *the Source* encourages us to be comfortable with not knowing everything.

This openness to uncertainty allows us to see beyond rigid beliefs and to approach each experience with fresh eyes.

When we let go of the need for absolute certainty, we create space for discovery. We allow ourselves to encounter new ideas, people, and possibilities without the pressure of fitting them into pre-existing beliefs.

This sense of curiosity and wonder aligns us more

closely with *the Source*, fostering a willingness to engage with life's mysteries rather than attempting to solve them all at once.

Practical Steps to See Beyond the Filters and Embrace Complexity

To apply these concepts in daily life, here are some practices to help you see beyond filters and embrace the complexity of truth:

1 . **Pause and Reflect**:
When you form a quick judgment or feel confident about a perspective, take a moment to pause.

Ask yourself if there might be other ways of seeing the situation. This small act can open the door to new insights.

2. **Question Assumptions**:
Gently challenge your beliefs by asking, "Why do I see things this way?" or "Is this the only way to interpret this?"

This practice can reveal your filters and help you

expand beyond them.

3. **Seek Out Diverse Perspectives**:
Engage with people with different backgrounds, beliefs, or life experiences.

Listening to others without judgment fosters empathy and encourages a more flexible approach to understanding.

4 . **Embrace Not Knowing**:
When faced with something you don't fully understand, try to accept the uncertainty.

Allowing space for questions rather than answers can lead to deeper insights over time, helping you grow more aligned with the wisdom of *the Source*.

5 . **Reflect on Multiple Truths**:
In situations where different truths appear to coexist, reflect on the possibility that both perspectives may hold value.

This approach respects the diversity of human experience and reminds us that truth is often layered, inviting us to see beyond the surface.

Conclusion: The Path to Clarity

Seeing beyond the filters and embracing the complexity of truth is a gradual, ongoing journey. As we become more aware of our perspectives and biases, we become more open to life's richness and diversity.

The Source is a constant reminder that reality is far more expansive than we often realise, urging us to remain curious and receptive.

Accepting that truth is multifaceted helps us develop a deeper connection to ourselves and the world around us.

By inviting us to see beyond our initial perceptions, *the Source* helps us move through life with compassion, understanding, and a profound respect for the many layers of reality.

A Final Reflection

Parting Wisdom for the Path Ahead

As we end this journey together, I hope these pages have offered you new insights and tools for connecting more deeply with *the Source*, bringing you closer to a life of purpose and fulfilment.

You've read about my experiences and the lessons I've learned, not to suggest a single way to live but to share how, through exploring these ideas, I've discovered a greater sense of meaning. I hope that, in your way, these insights resonate with you as you walk your unique path.

Throughout this book, we've explored the nature of

existence, the power of intention, and how our souls work in harmony with *the Source*. We've looked at how to create a life aligned with our true selves and how to manifest experiences that bring us joy, growth, and understanding.

Here are some of the core principles and practices that can serve as guideposts on your journey:

1. **Embracing Acts of Kindness and Paying It Forward**

By embracing random acts of kindness and choosing to "pay it forward," you create a ripple effect of positivity that uplifts others and yourself. These acts don't need to be grand—they might be as simple as a kind word, a helping hand, or a moment of patience.

When we move through life with kindness as our default, we cultivate abundance that flows through us and to others.

2. **Win When Nobody Loses**

One of the most potent ways to connect with *the Source* is through integrity—living with a "win-win" mindset where your success doesn't come at someone else's expense.

This approach nurtures balance, harmony, and authenticity, aligning your intentions with a collective good that supports everyone's growth.

3. **Accepting Life's Detours: A to B via C**

Life rarely takes us directly from one point to the next. Often, we find ourselves detouring through unexpected experiences—"Point C."

While sometimes frustrating, these detours are essential for our growth, equipping us with the wisdom, resilience, and insight to navigate life's challenges and blessings fully.

Trusting this process allows us to see each step as purposeful, even if it feels indirect.

4. **Understanding Rolling Roadblocks**

Sometimes, *the Source* presents delays or distractions to slow us down, helping us arrive at the right place and time. These "rolling roadblocks" might seem inconvenient, but they're often protective, helping us align with opportunities genuinely meant for us.

Trusting in divine timing means accepting these moments with patience and faith, knowing they're part of a more excellent plan.

5. **Choosing with Free Will**

The Source respects your free will; sometimes, it may present multiple paths, challenging you to choose based on your deepest desires. Every choice is an opportunity to affirm who you are and what you genuinely want, deepening your alignment with your soul's purpose.

Learning to navigate these choices with intuition strengthens your connection to *the Source* and keeps you on a path that feels genuinely yours.

A Simple Rule for Manifestation

If there's one guiding principle that captures the spirit of these pages, it's this:

Wake up daily, identify what excites you, and invest your energy, passion, and focus wholeheartedly.

Let your soul's intuition, not the mind's logical plans, guide you. True passion flows from a place of inner alignment, so trust this natural pull without overthinking the outcome.

The Source works through these moments of inspiration, nudging you toward experiences that bring you fulfilment.

The Source often nudges us with opportunities that respect our free will, allowing us to choose with clarity and authenticity. In these choices, we are invited to live in alignment with our most authentic selves.

The Journey Continues

The path of growth and self-discovery is only partially complete. If you're curious about how my journey unfolds, you can follow updates and insights at guidedbythesource.com.

I'll continue sharing my experiences and reflections, hoping they will encourage you to trust your path.

Thank you for joining me on this journey. If this book brings even a tiny moment of clarity, peace, or encouragement to just one person, then every hour spent writing it will have been worth it.

Stay connected to your intuition, nurture your passion, and trust that *the Source* is always guiding you.

I wish you a journey filled with blessings, love, and endless possibilities.

With gratitude,

Philip Brian Tomlinson

Joining the Guided by the Source Community

Walking the Path Together

As you've read this book, I hope its message has resonated with you. This journey isn't just mine; it's one we can share.

The insights here are seeds meant to grow in a community of like-minded people—a space where we can support, inspire, and grow together.

I've created *Guided by the Source*, an online community for those drawn to this message.

What the Community Offers

By joining the *Guided by the Source* community, you can:

•**Connect with Like-Minded People**: Share your reflections and experiences in a supportive space.

•**Ask Questions Directly**: Submit questions for me to answer.

•**Access Live Streams**: Join live sessions on our YouTube channel, exploring the book's themes and more.

•**Enjoy Exclusive Perks**: From early access to new content to shaping future projects, membership brings unique opportunities.

How Your Support Helps

This work is my calling, but it's also a mission that requires resources to sustain and grow. By joining the membership system, you're supporting more content creation, expanding the message, and helping others discover the guidance shared here.

Your contribution isn't just financial—it's a way to be part of something larger, a movement rooted in kindness, growth, and connection.

A Shared Journey

This isn't about following me—it's about walking together as a community. Whether you join as a member or connect with the message, know you're part of this journey.

Thank you for allowing me to share this work with you. Let's keep moving forward, guided always by the Source.

Visit GuidedbytheSource.com

To join the community, explore membership, and stay connected, visit guidedbythesource.com

Printed in Great Britain
by Amazon

7864920c-c024-4fcd-ba60-7b4a297f1021R01